The Prison Letters

Studies In Paul's Prison Epistles:

Ephesians
Philippians
Colossians
Philemon

By
Terry Kinard

TABLE OF CONTENTS

INTRODUCTION: The Prison Epistles — 4

PART ONE: Paul's Letter to the Ephesians — 6
- 1.1 The City of Ephesus — 6
- 1.2 Highlights in Ephesus — 7
- 1.3 Historical Setting — 7
- 1.4 Key Verse — 8
- 1.5 Theme — 8
- 1.6 Analysis — 10
- 1.7 Text — 12
  - Chapter One — 12
  - Note #1 Spiritual Blessings — 15
  - Note #2 Paul's Prayer — 17
  - Chapter Two — 18
  - Note #3 Relationship to Christ — 23
  - Chapter Three Outline — 24
  - Chapter Three — 25
  - Chapter Four — 29
  - Chapter Five — 35
  - Husbands and Wives — 38
  - Chapter Six — 42
  - Parents and Children — 42
  - Masters and Servants — 44
  - Spiritual War — 46
  - Note #4 Activities of Spiritual Wickedness — 48
  - Note #5 Seven Pieces of Armor — 50
  - Note #6 Work of the Holy Spirit — 52
  - Note #7 Christ's Love for the Church — 53

PART TWO: Paul's Letter to the Philippians — 54
- 2.1 The City of Philippi — 54
- 2.2 Overview of the Philippian Letter — 55
- 2.3 Historical Setting of the Philippian Letter — 55
- 2.4 Key Verse — 57
- 2.5 Text — 58
  - Chapter One — 58
  - Chapter Two — 62
  - Chapter Three — 66
  - Chapter Four — 69
  - Note #8 Eight Positive Areas of Thinking — 71
  - Note #9 Progression of a Transformed Life — 71

PART THREE: Paul's Letter to the Colossians	74
3.1 The City of Colosse	74
3.2 Historical Setting	75
Note #10 – Three Marks of a Cult	75
3.3 Comparison of Colossian and Ephesian letters	76
Note #11 – Corresponding verses in Colossians and Ephesians	76
3.4 Text	77
Chapter One	77
Chapter Two	82
Chapter Three	86
Chapter Four	90
PART FOUR: Paul's Letter to Philemon	93
4.1 Historical Setting	93
4.2 Overview	94
4.3 Analysis	95
4.4 Text	95
BIBLIOGRAPHY	100

INTRODUCTION TO THE PRISON LETTERS

Ephesians, Philippians, Colossians, and Philemon are collectively known as the Prison Epistles, because it is believed that the Apostle Paul wrote them during his first imprisonment in Rome, approximately A.D. 61-64. Exact times, locations and dates are not known.

Acts 28:16, 30-31
And when we came to Rome, the centurion delivered the prisoners to the captain of the guard: but Paul was suffered to dwell by himself with a soldier that kept him. (30) And Paul dwelt two whole years in his own hired house, and received all that came in unto him, (31) Preaching the kingdom of God, and teaching those things which concern the Lord Jesus Christ, with all confidence, no man forbidding him."

Most scholars agree there is ample evidence that Paul wrote these four letters about the same time:

1. The same messenger, Tychicus, delivered both the Colossians and the Ephesian letters.

    Colossians 4:7-10
    All my state shall Tychicus declare unto you, who is a beloved brother, and a faithful minister and fellow servant in the Lord: (8) Whom I have sent unto you for the same purpose, that he might know your estate, and comfort your hearts; (9) With Onesimus, a faithful and beloved brother, who is one of you (10) They shall make known unto you all things which are done here.

    Ephesians 6:21
    But that ye also may know my affairs, and how I do, Tychicus, a beloved brother and faithful minister in the Lord, shall make known to you all things: (22) Whom I have sent unto you for the same purpose, that ye might know our affairs, and that he might comfort your hearts.

2. The letters to Colosse and to Philemon were delivered by both Tychicus and Onesimus (the runaway servant of Philemon), SEE Colossians 4:7-9 above.

    Philemon 10,17
    I (Paul) beseech thee for my son Onesimus, whom I have begotten in my bonds: (17) If thou count me therefore a partner, receive him as myself.

3. <u>Paul wrote the Philippians using the phrases "my bonds" and "Caesar's household," as well as expressing his hope of being released.</u>

   Philippians 1:7, 13,14,16,17
   Even as it is meet for me to think this of you all, because I have you in my heart; inasmuch as both in my bonds, and in the defense and confirmation of the gospel, ye all are partakers of my grace. (13) So that my bonds in Christ are manifest in all the palace, and in all other places; (14) And many of the brethren in the Lord, waxing confident by my bonds, are much more bold to speak the word without fear. (16) The one preach Christ of contention, not sincerely, supposing to add affliction to my bonds (17) but the other of love, knowing that I am set for the defense of the gospel.

PART ONE

PAUL'S LETTER TO THE EPHESIANS

> AUTHOR: Paul
>
> DATE: Early 60s A.D. during Paul's first Roman imprisonment
>
> THEME: Nature, purpose and unity of The Church
>
> The early Christian Jews tended to be unwilling to fellowship with their Gentile brothers in the faith. Paul may have written to the church at Ephesus to teach them about God's plan for unity among believers.
>
> WRITTEN TO: Ephesus, probably as a circular letter for all churches of Asia
>
> OTHER KEY PEOPLE: Tychicus

SECTION 1.1 THE CITY OF EPHESUS

a. The capital of the province of Asia
b. The main port of Asia, located three miles inland on the Cayster River.
c. The most important commercial city that Paul visited.
d. Paul visited Ephesus on his second missionary journey while on his way to Jerusalem.

Acts 18:1,11, 18,19-21 After these things Paul departed from Athens and came to Corinth. (11) And he continued there a year and six months, teaching the word of God among them. (18) And Paul after this tarried there yet a good while, and then took his leave of the brethren, and sailed thence into Syria, and wit him Priscilla and Aquila; having shorn his head in Cenchrea: for he had a vow. (19) And he came to Ephesus, and left them there: but he himself entered into the synagogue, and reasoned with the Jews. (20)When they desired him to tarry longer time with them, he consented not; (21) But bade them farewell, saying, I must by all means keep this feast that cometh in Jerusalem: but I will return again unto you, if God will. And he sailed from Ephesus.

e. Later, on his third missionary journey, Paul stayed in Ephesus three years.

Acts 20:31 [In Miletus, meeting with the Ephesian church elders] Therefore watch, and remember, that by the space of three years I ceased not to warn every one night and day with tears.

SECTION 1:2   HIGHLIGHTS IN EPHESUS

    a. Acts 19:1-7 Twelve disciples of John the Baptist were baptized in water and in the Holy Spirit

    b. Acts 19:8-10 Paul preached in the synagogues and taught in the school of Tyrannus
    c. Acts 19:11-12 Special miracles were done by God through Paul

    d. Acts 19:13-17 Evil spirits recognized Paul

    e. Acts 19:18-20 New converts burned their books and magic charms
    f. Acts 19:21-41 Paul's preaching caused a riot by worshipers of the goddess Diana

    g. Acts 20:17-38 Paul spoke to Ephesian church elders for last time

    h. Revelation 2:1-4 John wrote to Ephesus a rebuke about leaving its first love

SECTION 1.3 HISTORICAL SETTING

The church in Ephesus was established in A.D. 53 on Paul's homeward journey to Jerusalem. He returned a year later, on his third missionary trip, and stayed there for three years, preaching and teaching with great effectiveness (Acts 19:1-20). Later, Paul met with the Ephesian leaders and sent Timothy to serve as their leader (I Timothy 1:3). A few years later, Paul was sent as a prisoner t Rom. While there, he was visited by several leaders from various places, among them Tychicus of Ephesus. Paul wrote the letter to the Ephesians and sent it by Tychicus to be distributed to all the churches in Asia.

The original Greek does not include the words "in Ephesus" in Ep 1:1. Nor does Paul include personal greetings, which is unusual in view of the fact that he spent over three years with the Ephesian church, and was very close to them.He also did not mention any personal problems in the church or situations peculiar to the area. It is probable, therefore, that the letter was written to instruct and encourage all the churches in Asia, and intended to be circulated. As the hub of the area, the Ephesian church sent the letter out by messenger, and thus it became known as the letter to the Ephesians.

Paul wrote to the Ephesian church while under "house arrest" in Rome (Acts 28:16). He had served the Lord for nearly 30 years, taken three missionary trips, and established churches throughout the area surrounding the Mediterranean Sea.

SECTION 1.4 KEY VERSE:

Ephesians 4:13
"Till we all come in the unity of the faith, and of the knowledge of the Son of God, unto a perfect man unto the measure of the stature of the fullness of Christ"

SECTION 1:5 THE THEME OF UNITY (with emphasis to Jew and Gentile believers):

a. The use of the word "together"

    Ep 1:10 …he might gather together in one…

    Ep 2:5 …hath quickened us together

    Ep 2:6 hath raised us up together, …made us sit together

    Ep 2:22 …ye also are builded together for a habitation of God

b. The use of the word "one"

    Ep 2:15 one new man

    Ep 2:16 one body

    Ep 2:18 one Spirit

    Ep 4:4 one Hope

    Ep 4:5 One Lord, one faith, one baptism

    Ep 4:6 One God and Father of all

c. The use of the phrase "in Christ"

    Ep 1:1,3,6,12,15,20

    Ep 2:10, 13

    Ep 3:11

    Ep 4:21

d. The use of the phrase "in heavenly places"

    Ep 1:3,20

    Ep 2:6

    Ep 3:10

e. The use of the word "riches"

    Ep 1:7, 2:7, riches of grace

    Ep 1:18, 3:16, riches of glory

    Ep 3:8, riches of Christ

SECTION 1:6 ANALYSIS

    a. Chapters 1,2, and 3 are DOCTRINAL, the believer's WEALTH in Christ. The first half of the book opens with the source of the believer's wealth:

    Ephesians 1:3 "Blessed be the God and Father of our Lord Jesus Christ, who hath blessed us with all spiritual blessings in heavenly places in Christ."

    b. Chapters 4,5, and 6 are PRACTICAL, the believer's WALK in Christ. The second half of the book opens with the exhortation to believers to walk with Christ.

    Ephesians 4:1 "I therefore, the prisoner of the Lord, beseech you that ye walk worthy of the vocation wherewith ye are called."

FIRST HALF OF BOOK breaks by chapters, each complete in itself and part of whole

    c. Chapter One:

        1. Spiritual Possessions (3-14)
        2. Spiritual Perceptions (15-23)

    d. Chapter Two:

        1. Gift of Salvation through Christ (1-10)
        2. Relationship in Him (11-22)

    e. Chapter Three:

        1. Mystery of God's Plan (1-12)
        2. Prayer for God's Fullness (13-21)

SECOND HALF OF BOOK (chpts 4-6) BREAKS BY TOPIC

    f. Chapter 4:1-16: Walking in relation to the Church

    g. Chapter 4:17 – 5:2 Walking in relation to Self

    i. Chapter 5:3-21 Walking in relation to worldly Outsiders

    j. Chapter 5:22-6:9 Walking in relation to Family
       (wives, husbands, children, parents, servants, masters)

    k. Chapter 6:10-20 Walking in Warfare against satanic powers

    l. Chapter 6:21-24 Conclusion and Paul's closing Prayer

SECTION 1.7 TEXT: PAUL'S LETTER TO THE EPHESIANS

CHAPTER ONE:

The Blessings of Redemption

1:1 Paul, an apostle of Jesus Christ by the will of God, to the saints which are at Ephesus, and to the faithful in Christ Jesus:

1:2 Grace be to you, and peace, from God our Father, and from the Lord Jesus Christ.

a. Paul pointed out that he was an apostle by God's will. He did not call himself into ministry.

b. Paul preached at Ephesus on his second missionary journey, and returned on his third missionary journey. He stayed in Ephesus longer than anywhere else, almost three years (Acts 20:31).

c. Ephesus was one of the five major cities in the Roman empire. The others were: Rome, Corinth, Antioch, and Alexandria.

d. Ephesus was a commercial, political, and religious center for Asia Minor, in what is now known as Turkey. Through the city of Ephesus Paul was able to evangelize all of Asia Minor.

e. Ephesus was the home of the temple of the Greek goddess Artemis, the many-breasted idol which was worshipped through prostitution. Artemis was known as the goddess "Diana" to the Romans.

f. "To the faithful in Christ Jesus" could refer to the fact that the letter was to be circulated throughout all the churches in the area. It could also refer to a group within the church, the "core" group of faithful Christians who were more dedicated, such as can be found in almost every congregation. There are always those who do the bulk of the work.

g. The term "in Christ Jesus" is a phrase use over 130 times in the New Testament. It describes our vital union with our Savior.

h. "Grace" and "peace" are given by God and received by His children by faith. They can be multiplied through knowledge (2 Peter 1:2).

1:3 Blessed be the God and Father of our Lord Jesus Christ, who hath blessed us with all spiritual blessings in heavenly places in Christ:

    a. Verses 3-14 contain the longest outpouring of praise in Paul's letters

    b. "Hath blessed us" indicates past tense action. The Greek is in the aorist tense, which means these blessings were obtained at a point in time and given to us. The victory has already been won! "It is finished" (John 19:30).

1:4 According as he hath chosen us in him before the foundation of the world, that we should be holy and without blame before him in love:

    a. "chosen us" – is in the aorist tense meaning "once for all".

    b. "chosen" has preposition "ek" prefixed, which means "out of"

    c. "chosen" is the middle voice of the verb which means to choose for oneself

    d. We are chosen "out of" the world, "once for all" to be God's own as a peculiar treasure!

1:5 Having predestinated us unto the adoption of children by Jesus Christ to himself, according to the good pleasure of his will,

    a. To be "adopted" (in New Testament Greek) means the public attestation of adult sonship

    b. Adopted infers the conferring of the privileges belonging to sons who have come to be of legal age.

1:6 To the praise of the glory of his grace, wherein he hath made us accepted in the beloved.

1:7 In whom we have redemption through his blood, the forgiveness of sins, according to the riches of his grace;

    a. To redeem is to buy back (but not a ransom to the devil).

    b. The redemption price answered the holy law of God (Ga 3:13)

    c. We are redeemed from the penalty we deserved (I Co 6:20)

    d. The payment for our freedom – His blood.

1:8 Wherein he hath abounded toward us in all wisdom and prudence;

1:9 Having made known unto us the mystery of his will, according to his good pleasure which he hath purposed in himself:

1:10 That in the dispensation of the fullness of times he might gather together in one all things in Christ, both which are in heaven, and which are on earth; even in him:

    a. "Fullness of times" looks beyond all things to the ages to come (Ep 2:7)

    b. There shall be the "throne of God and the Lamb"(Re 22:3).

1:11 In whom also we have obtained an inheritance, being predestinated according to the purpose of him who worketh all things after the counsel of his own will:

1:12 That we should be to the praise of his glory, who first trusted in Christ.

    a. We have our inheritance "in Him" who is heir to all!

    b. "His own will" indicates no power can overcome or stop His purpose

1:13 In whom ye also trusted after that ye heard the word of truth, the gospel of your salvation in whom also after that ye believed, ye were sealed with that Holy Spirit of promise,

1:14 Which is the earnest of our inheritance until the redemption of the purchased possession, unto the praise of his glory.

    a. God's "sealing" us by His Spirit is the security of the believer.

    b. He bought us (owns us) and seals us (secures us).

Note #1: SIX SPIRITUAL BLESSINGS:

1. Election

2. Predestination

3. Redemption

4. Revelation

5. Inheritance

6. Sealing of the Spirit

1:15 Wherefore I also, after I heard of your faith in the Lord Jesus, and love unto all the saints,

      a. Verse 15 marks a transition from Praise (vs 3-14, for spiritual Possession)

      b. To Prayer (v 15-23, for spiritual Perception)

1:16 Cease no to give thanks for you, making mention of you in my prayers;

1:17 That the God of our Lord Jesus Christ, the Father of glory, may give unto you the spirit of wisdom and revelation in the knowledge of him:

1:18 The eyes of your understanding being enlightened; that ye may know what is the hope of his calling, and what the riches of the glory of his inheritance in the saints,

1:19 And what is the exceeding greatness of his power to us-ward who believe, according to the working of mighty power.

1:20 Which he wrought in Christ, when he raised him from the dead, and set him at his own right hand in the heavenly places,

1:21 Far above al principality, and power, and might, and dominion, and every name that is named, not only in this world, but also in that which is to come:

1:22 And hath put all things under his feet, and gave him to be the head over all things to the church,

1:23 Which is his body, the fullness of him that filleth all in all.

Note #2: PAUL'S PRAYER

1. Know what is the hope of His calling

    "Calling" = the work of God's grace in our hearts, our conversion

    "Hope" = the end of our faith, the ultimate prize

2. Know the riches of His inheritance in the saints

    "In the saints" means that God finds an inheritance in us, through Christ. Israel was God's inheritance in the Old Testament (De 4:20; I Ki 8:53)

3. Know the exceeding greatness of His power to usward who believe

    a. "His power" to us is according to what God did in Jesus Christ.

    b. God raised Jesus Christ from the dead by His mighty power.

    c. All of Hell could not prevent the resurrection of Jesus Christ.

    d. Paul prays for a spiritual knowing (revelation) of God's power in us.

CHAPTER TWO

Salvation

2:1 And you hath he quickened, who were dead in trespasses and sins;

2:2 Wherein in time past ye walked according to the course of this world, according to the prince of the power of the air, the spirit that now worketh in the children of disobedience:

2:3 Among whom also we all had our conversation in times past in the lusts of our flesh, fulfilling the desires of the flesh and of the mind; and were by nature the children of wrath, even as others.

    a. Ep 2:1 Our new condition in Christ – saved

    b. Ep 2:2-5 Our previous condition outside of Christ – lost (4 characteristics)

        a. "dead in trespasses and sins" – spiritual death

        b. "walked according to course of this world" – satanic control

        c. "fulfilling the desires of the flesh and of the mind" – sense (flesh) control

        d. "were by nature the children of wrath" – from Hebrew idiom meaning under "sentence" of wrath (example, SEE I Sa 20:31). New Testament, SEE 2 Pe 2:14; Ma 23:15; Jn 27:12).

2:4 But God, who is rich in mercy, for his great love wherewith he loved us,

    "BUT GOD"- This changes the tone emphatically to the GOOD NEWS of the GOSPEL!

2:5 Even when we were dead in sins, hath quickened us together with Christ, (by grace ye are saved;)

    a. We were dead in sins, BUT GOD has quickened us together with Christ

    b. Demonstration of God's divine POWER (who else could do it) and

    c. GRACE (who else would do it)

    d. God's first step toward us – making us spiritually alive!

2:6 And hath raised us up together, and made us sit together in heavenly places in Christ Jesus:

    a. AND GOD ALSO "raised us up together…in Christ"

    b. As Jesus was raised in victory over Satan, we too are not only given life, but also given freedom. Satan is under our feet!

    c. AND GOD ALSO "made us sit together in heavenly places in Christ"

        a. Our eyes are opened to spiritual truths

        b. Our minds think spiritual thoughts

        c. Our hearts experience spiritual joys

        d. Our life experiences spiritual privileges

        e. Our choice should be to live in this spiritual experience

2:7 That in the ages to come he might show the exceeding riches of his grace in his kindness toward us through Christ Jesus.

    a. AND GOD ALSO showed the "exceeding riches of his grace"

    b. AND GOD ALSO showed (exceeding riches) "in his kindness toward us"

    c. AND GOD ALSO showed his commitment to us "in the ages to come"!

2:8 For by grace are ye saved through faith; and that not of yourselves: it is the gift of God:

2:9 Not of works, lest any man should boast.

2:10 For we are his workmanship, created in Christ Jesus unto good works, which God hath before ordained that we should walk in them.

- a. Paul emphasizes the abundance of grace by twice proclaiming in this passage "By grace are ye saved!" (verses 5 and 8)

- b. Paul emphasizes salvation is "not of works, lest any man should boast"

- c. Verses 1-10 contrast who we are in Christ and who we were before Christ

2:11 Wherefore remember, that ye being in time past Gentiles in the flesh, who are called Uncircumcision by that which is called the Circumcision in the flesh made by hands;

2:12 That at that time ye were without Christ, being aliens from the commonwealth of Israel, and strangers from the covenants of promise, having no hope, and without God in the world.

- a. "At that time ye were"

    - a. "without Christ" (outside Israel's privilege)

    - b. "aliens from the commonwealth of Israel" (no inheritance w/Israel)

    - c. "strangers from the covenants of promise" (no share by birth)

    - d. "no hope" (apart from Messiah/Savior)

    - e. "without God in the world" (without true knowledge of God)

2:13 But now in Christ Jesus ye who sometimes were far off are made nigh by the blood of Christ.

2:14 For he is our peace, who hath made both one, and hath broken down the middle wall of partition between us;

2:15 Having abolished in his flesh the enmity, even the law of commandments contained in ordinances; for to make in himself of twain one new man, so making peace;

2:16 And that he might reconcile both unto God in one body by the cross, having slain the enmity thereby:

2:17 And came and preached peace to you which were afar off, and to them that were nigh.

2:18 For through him we both have access by one Spirit unto the Father.

      a. "BUT NOW in Christ Jesus" All is made new

          1. "far off are made nigh"

          2. "he is our peace, who hath made both one (Jew and Gentile)

          3. "hath broken down the middle wall of partition" (unity)

          4. "abolished …the enmity…so making peace"

2:19 Now therefore ye are no more strangers and foreigners, but fellow citizens with the saints, and of the household of God;

2:20 And are built upon the foundation of the apostles and prophets, Jesus Christ himself being the chief corner stone;

2:21 In whom all the building fitly framed together groweth unto a holy temple in the Lord:

2:22 In whom ye also are builded together for a habitation of God through the Spirit.

    a. "Now therefore" (more emphasis on our position and privilege through relationship with God through Jesus Christ

        a. "fellow-citizens of the city of God"

        b. "fellow-citizens of the household (family) of God"

        c. all "built upon the (single) foundation

        d. all built together into "a holy

        e. all built "through the Spirit"

Note #3: Relationship to Christ

The Old Relationship (verses 11-12) "at that time ye were"

    1.

    2.

    3.

    4.

    5.

The New Relationship (verses 19-22) "Now therefore ye are"

    1.

    2.

    3.

    4.

    5.

How the Change was Purchased (verses 13-18) "But now in Christ Jesus"

    1.

    2.

    3.

    4.

    5.

    6.

    7.

    8.

CHAPTER THREE OUTLINE

1. One of the most profound chapters in the Bible.

2. The Divine mystery (verses 1-12)

    a. This secret was not the Gospel, but is IN the Gospel.

    b. The Gospel was foretold by the prophets and was NO SECRET

       a. Christ would come

       b. Christ would bear the sins of many

       c. Christ would be a Prince and Savior to both Jew and Gentile

       d. Christ would pour out the Holy Spirit

       e. Christ would preach/commission preaching of remission of sin

       f. Christ should take the throne of David

    c. The Mystery or Secret "hid in God" was the divine purpose to create THE CHURCH from both Jew and Gentile

    d. The Divine provision (verses 13-21)

       f. "Wherefore..." Paul explains why Christians should be strong.

       g. His prayer in Chapter One was that we may "KNOW"

       h. His prayer in Chapter Three was that we may "HAVE"

CHAPTER THREE

God's Plan

3:1 For this cause I Paul, the prisoner of Jesus Christ for you Gentiles,

    a. *"the prisoner of Jesus Christ" shows Paul's mindset and perspective*

    b. *SEE Ep 4:1; 2 Ti 1:8; Phile 1:9; Ep 6:20*

    c. *Paul knew he was persecuted for righteousness' sake, not any sin of his own*

    d. *God used Paul's trials as catalyst to get him to Rome to preach*

3:2 If ye have heard of the dispensation of the grace of God which is given me to you-ward.

    a. *"dispensation" also translated "stewardship"-responsibility for another's property (Thayer)*

    b. *God gave Paul understanding of GRACE to give to others through him*

3:3 How that by revelation he made known unto me the mystery; (as I wrote afore in few words,

3:4 Whereby, when ye read, ye may understand my knowledge in the mystery of Christ.)

3:5 Which is other ages was not made known unto the sons of men, as it is now revealed unto his holy apostles and prophets by the Spirit;

3:6 That the Gentiles should be fellow heirs, and of the same body, and partakers of the promise in Christ by the gospel:

3:7 Whereof I was made a minister, according to the gift of the grace of God given unto me by the effectual working of his power.

3:8 Unto me, who am less than the least of all saints, is this grace given, tht I should preach among the Gentiles the unsearchable riches of Christ;

3:9 And to make all men see what is the fellowship of the mystery, which from the beginning of the world hath been hid in God, who created all things by Jesus Christ:

    a. "the mystery" – Dictionaries define "Mystery" as a secret, or something unknown, unexplained

    b. The mystery Paul speaks of is the mystery of the Church, Jew and Gentile as joint-heirs with Jesus Christ

3:10 To the intent that now unto the principalities and powers in heavenly places might be known by the church the manifold wisdom of God,

3:11 According to the eternal purpose which he purposed in Christ Jesus our Lord:

3:12 In whom we have boldness and access with confidence by the faith of him.

    a. Paul spoke by revelation more than he could imagine, for the church from his day until this day are hearing, believing and receiving the mystery of God's plan for the Church

    b. The mystery is repeated in Colossians 1:27 "Christ in you the hope of glory."

3:13 Wherefore I desire that ye faint not at my tribulations for you, which is your glory.

    a. Paul refers to his imprisonment

    b. Paul follows with a prayer for their strength

3:14 For this cause I bow my knees unto the Father of our Lord Jesus Christ,

3:15 Of whom the whole family in heaven and earth is named,

3:16 That he would grant you, according to the riches of his glory, to be strengthened with might by his Spirit in the inner man;

    a. "strengthened with might by his Spirit in the inner man" – Our strength is by the Spirit of God

    b. "That" in verses 16,17,19 in Greek = conjunction "hina"= "in order that"

3:17 That Christ may dwell in your hearts by faith; that ye, being rooted and grounded in love,

    a. "rooted and grounded in love" -Our security is in the love of God

3:18 May be able to comprehend with all saints what is the breadth, and length, and depth, and height;

3:19 And to know the love of Christ, which passeth knowledge, that ye might be filled with all the fullness of God.

    a. "filled with all the fullness of God" – Our victory is in the fullness of God

    b. The "fullness of God" in Christ Himself! (Ep 1:22-23;Co 1:19; 2:9-10)

    c. To be filled with God is to be filled with Jesus Christ!

    d. "with" in Revised Version is "unto"- "all" = completeness, to our utmost capacity to be possessed and filled by Him

    e. A seemingly impossible prayer – completely filled with His life!

3:20 Now unto him that is able to do exceeding abundantly above all that we ask or think, according to the power that worketh in us,

    a. God has all power to do whatever He wishes, but it is tied to the power that works in us

3:21 Unto him be glory in the church by Christ Jesus throughout all ages, world without end. Amen.

    a. He is able to not only fill us to capacity with Himself, but to do so "exceeding abundantly above…

    b. according to the power (His) that worketh (eth=continuous action) in us

CHAPTER FOUR

Unity of Believers

4:1 I therefore, the prisoner of the Lord, beseech you that ye walk worthy of the vocation wherewith ye are called,

    a. WALK - "Walk worthy of the vocation" – totally committed

    b. Ep 2:10 "created in Christ Jesus unto good works, which God hath before ordained that we should walk in them."

4:2 With all lowliness and meekness, with longsuffering, forbearing one another in love;

    a. Four virtues of the Christian life:

        1. _____

        2. _____

        3. _____

        4. _____

4:3 Endeavoring to keep the unity of the Spirit in the bond of peace.

    a. We are all one in Christ Jesus and should strive (be determined) to live in peace

    b. We will all spend eternity together "as in Heaven" (Mt :10)

4:4 There is one body, and one Spirit, even as ye are called in one hope of your calling;

4:5 One Lord, one faith, one baptism,

4:6 One God and Father of all, who is above all, and through all, and in you all.

    a. Unity, "one" (vs 4-6)

    b. God is over all, through all, in all –overruling care – transcendence

    c. God's Presence is active in the earth –active presence - immanence

4:7 But unto every one of us is given grace according to the measure of the gift of Christ.

    a. Each of us has gifts, "as Christ apportioned it" (Life App. Bible, NIV)

    b. Each of us has gifts…to contribute to the whole body of Christ

4:8 Wherefore he saith, When he ascended up on high, he led captivity captive, and gave gifts unto men.

    a. "led captivity captive" refers to Jesus' liberation of Old Testament saints

    b. "gave gifts unto men" refers to ministry gifts (SEE vs 11)

4:9 (Now that he ascended, what is it but that he also descended first into the lower parts of the earth?

    a. "lower parts of the earth" refers to "sheol" (Hebrew)

    b. place in heart of the earth where spirits of men went before Jesus' crucifixion

4:10 He that descended is the same also that ascended up far above all heavens, that he might fill all things.)

    a. Jesus went to "sheol," was resurrected, and ascended to heaven

    b. "fill all things" refers to fulfilling all prophecies

4:11 And he gave some, apostles; and some prophets; and some, evangelists; and some, pastors and teachers;

4:12 For the perfecting of the saints, for the work of the ministry, for the edifying of the body of Christ:

4:13 Till we all come in the unity of the faith, and of the knowledge of the Son of God, unto a perfect man, unto the measure of the statue of the fullness of Christ:

4:14 That we henceforth be no more children, tossed to and fro, and carried about with every wind of doctrine, by the sleight of men, and cunning craftiness, whereby they lie in wait to deceive;

4:15 But speaking the truth in love, may grown up into him in all things, which is the head, even Christ:

    a. God's purpose is that Christians mature in their faith.

    b. God's ministry gifts testify that He expects the Church to grow up.

    c. "speaking the truth in love" is the mark of maturity

4:16 From whom the whole body fitly joined together and compacted by that which every joint supplieth, according to the effectual working in the measure of every part, maketh increase of the body unto the edifying of itself in love.

    a. God gives ministry gifts to men

    b. Ministers are gifts from God to the Church, the Body of Christ

    c. Ministers are to equip the saints, who do the work of the ministry

4:17 This I say therefore, and testify in the Lord, that ye henceforth walk not as other Gentiles walk, in the vanity of their mind,

4:18 Having the understanding darkened, being alienated from the life of God through the ignorance that is in them, because of the blindness of their heart:

4:19 Who being past feeling have given themselves over unto lasciviousness, to work all uncleanness with greediness.

4:20 But ye have not so learned Christ;

4:21 If so be that yea have heard him, and have been taught by him, as the truth is in Jesus:

    a. Ep 4:17-20 describe how unbelievers live

    b. Vs 20 makes it clear that followers of Christ do not live like unbelievers

4:22 That ye put off concerning the former conversation the old man, which is corrupt according to the deceitful lusts;

4:23 And be renewed in the spirit of your mind;

4:24 And that ye put on the new man, which after God is created in righteousness and true holiness.

    a. Ep 4:22-24 speak of putting off the former manner of conduct (like unbelievers live) which was the result of the "old man" or "old nature" which is part of the old

    b. "ye put off", "(you) be renewed", "you put on" refers to "clothing oneself, sink into (clothing) (Thayer)

4:25 Wherefore putting away lying, speak every man truth with his neighbor: for we are members one of another.

    a. "wherefore" means because of this

    b. practical "how to's" follow through vs 29

4:26 Be ye angry, and sin not: let not the sun go down upon your wrath:

4:27 Neither give place to the devil.

4:28 Let him that stole steal no more: but rather let him labor, working with his hands the thing which is good, that he may have to give to him that needeth.

4:29 Let no corrupt communication proceed out of your mouth, but that which is good to the use of edifying, that it may minister grace unto the hearers.

    a. Speak the truth (vs 25)

    b. Have godly anger, without sin (vs 26)

    c. Do not steal (vs 28)

    d. Speak to build up and encourage (vs 29)

4:30 And grieve not the Holy Spirit of God, whereby ye are sealed unto the day of redemption.

4:31 Let all bitterness, and wrath, and anger, and clamor, and evil speaking, be put away from you, with all malice:

4:32 And be ye kind one to another, tenderhearted, forgiving one another, even as God for Christ's sake hath forgiven you.

    a. The Holy Spirit is a Person who can be grieved.

    b. Ep 1:13 "ye were sealed with that Holy Spirit of promise"

    c. Ep 4:30 "grieve not the Holy Spirit…whereby ye are sealed unto the day"

    d. All evil listed (vs 25-31) grieve the Spirit of God

CHAPTER FIVE

Walk in Love

5:1 Be ye therefore followers of God as dear children:

5:2 And walk in love, as Christ also hath loved us, and hath given himself for us an offering and a sacrifice to Go for a sweet smelling savor.

5:3 But fornication, and all uncleanness, or covetousness, let it not be once named among you, as becometh saints;

5:4 Neither filthiness, nor foolish talking, nor jesting, which are not convenient: but rather giving of thanks.

5:5 For this ye know, that no whoremonger, nor unclean person, nor covetous man, who is an idolater, hath any inheritance in the kingdom of Christ and of God.

5:6 Let no man deceive you with vain words: for because of these things cometh the wrath of God upon the children of disobedience.

5:7 Be not ye therefore partakers with them.

5:8 For ye were sometimes darkness, but now are ye light in the Lord: <u>walk as children of light:</u>

    a. WALK in good works (Ep 2:10)

    b. WALK worthy of your calling (Ep 4:1)

    c. WALK no longer as Gentiles (Ep 4:17)

    d. WALK in love (Ep 5:2)

    e. WALK as children of light (Ep 5:8)

    f. WALK circumspectly (Ep 5:15)

5:9 (For the fruit of the Spirit is in all goodness and righteousness and truth;)

5:10 Proving what is acceptable unto the Lord.

5:11 And have no fellowship with the unfruitful works of darkness, but rather reprove them.

5:12 For it is a shame even to speak of those things which are done of them in secret.

5:13 But all things that are reproved are made manifest by the light: for whatsoever doth make manifest is light.

5:14 Wherefore he saith, Awake thou that sleepest, and arise from the dead, and Christ shall give thee light.

5:15 See then that ye <u>walk circumspectly</u>, not as fools, but as wise, SEE Ep 5:8 list

5:17 Wherefore be ye not unwise, but understanding what the will of the Lord is.

    a. "redeeming the time" – make the most of our time here

    b. "the will of the Lord" – salvation for all men is God's desire (freedom from sin, sickness, poverty, bondage of the devil)

    c. Understanding God's heart motivates us to walk like Him and redeem time

5:18 And be not drunk with wine, wherein is excess; but be filled with the Spirit;

5:19 Speaking to yourselves in psalms and hymns and spiritual songs, singing and making melody in your heart to the Lord;

    a. Do not get drunk with wine and "be filled with the Spirit" are both commands

    b. The Spirit-filled life is characterized by Worship

5:20 Giving thanks always for all things unto God and the Father in the name of our Lord Jesus Christ;

    a. Our worship should be full of thanksgiving, glorifying God, not our problems

    b. Hebrews 10:36 relates to I Thessalonians 5:18

Relationship: Husbands and Wives

5:21 Submitting yourselves one to another in the fear of God.

    a. Submission is two ways, not one.

    b. "in the fear of God" indicates submission to man is second to submission to God

5:22 Wives, submit yourselves unto your own husbands, as unto the Lord.

5:23 For the husband if the head of the wife, even as Christ is the head of the church: and he is the savior of the body.

5:24 Therefore as the church is subject unto Christ so let the wives be to their own husbands in every thing.

    a. There is a greater demand on the wife to submit, as her husband follows God

    b. In a partnership, someone has to have final say, and God has given that to the husband, as long as he is in line with the Lord

    c. SEE vs 21 "in the fear of God"

    d. Wives are not told to obey ungodliness

5:25 Husbands, love your wives, even as Christ also loved the church, and gave himself for it;

    a. Husbands are commanded to love, because naturally they do not tend to give the emotional support women need

    b. Wives are told to respect their husbands, because naturally they do not tend to give the respect husbands need

5:26 That he might sanctify and cleanse it with the washing of water by the word.

    a. "sanctify" means to set apart

    b. "cleanse" means to wash from filth

    c. "washing of water by the word" refers to the cleansing power of the Word of God (SEE Jn 15:3)

5:27 That he might present it to himself a glorious church, not having spot, or wrinkle, or any such things: but that it should be holy and without blemish.

    a. "glorious church" refers to the power of God in the Church, not human effort

    b. "holy and without blemish" is not possible through the flesh

    c. He presents the Church to Himself

5:28 So ought men to love their wives as their own bodies. He that loveth his wife loveth himself.

5:29 For no man ever yet hated his own flesh; but nourisheth and cherisheth it, even as the Lord the church.

    a. *vs* 25 Men are commanded to love their wives as Christ the Church

    b. vs 28 Men are commanded to love their wives as their own bodies

5:30 For we are members of his body, of his flesh, and of his bones.

5:31 For this cause shall a man leave his father and mother, and shall be joined unto his wife, and thy two shall be one flesh.

5:32 This is a great mystery: but I speak concerning Christ and the church.

5:33 Nevertheless let every one of you in particular so love his wife even as himself; and the wife see that she reverence her husband.

    a. Paul uses twice as many words telling husbands to love their wives, as he does telling wives to submit to their husbands.

    b. How does Paul tell men to love their wives? (Life Application Bible)

        1.

        2.

        3.

CHAPTER SIX

Relationships: Parents and Children

6:1 Children, obey your parents in the Lord: for this is right.

    a. Wives (vs 21-33) are told to submit. Children are told to obey.

    b. To obey means to do as one is told. Submit means to honor, respect, love

6:2 Honor thy father and mother; which is the first commandment with promise;

6:3 That it may be well with thee, and thou mayest live long on the earth.

    a. Children, young or adult, are not commanded to disobey God in order to obey parents.

    b. The command (6:1) is "in the Lord".

    c. First commandment with promise (SEE Exodus 20:12)

    d. The promise is long life and good life.

    e. Long life is a blessing, not a curse.

6:4 And, ye fathers, provoke not your children to wrath: but bring them up in the nurture and admonition of the Lord,

    a. "fathers, provoke not" – fathers are more prone to be stern than mothers, and thus provoke children to anger

    b. Parents are not to frustrate, insult, or discourage their children

    c. Parenting is not merely pointing out mistakes, but must minister love and positive statements.

Relationships: Masters and Servants
(Employers and Employees)

6:5 Servants, be obedient to them that are your masters according to the flesh, with fear and trembling, in singleness of your heart, as unto Christ;

6:6 Not with eyeservice, as menpleasers, but as the servants of Christ, doing the will of God from the heart.

6:7 With good will doing service, as to the Lord, and not to men.

6:8 Knowing that whatsoever good thing any man doeth, the same shall he receive of the Lord whether he be bond or free.

    a. Work as unto Christ. Always give it your best.

    b. Work as unto the Lord, for His approval, not man's.

  c. Paul did not address slavery, but took the approach that to change society, hearts must be changed by God. Trying to change men apart from heart issues causes rebellion and wars.

6:9 And, ye masters, do the same things unto them, forbearing threatening: knowing that your Master also is in heaven; neither is there respect of persons with him.

  a. Paul told employers not to intimidate employees.

  b. He who would be greatest must be servant of all (Mt 20:27)

  c. When we humble ourselves, God will exalt us (I Pe 5:6).

Spiritual Warfare
How to Live Victoriously in this Present World

6:10 Finally, my brethren, be strong in the Lord, and in the power of his might.

    a. Victory is in God's ability, not man's.

    b. Make the greatest trade: your life for His!

6:11 Put on the whole armor of God, that ye may be able to stand against the wiles of the devil.

    a. Be fully protected by taking on the "whole armor of God"

    b. Just helmet of salvation leaves you exposed to the devil's attacks.

    c. Jesus stripped Satan of his power and authority (Mt 28:18).

    d. The only power Satan has against us is deception.

6:12 For we wrestle not against flesh and blood, but against principalities, against powers, against the rulers of the darkness of this world, against spiritual wickedness in high places.

    a. Warfare is not against people, but against powers of darkness that work behind the scenes through people.

    b. Spiritual warfare requires spiritual weapons. Natural weapons will not work, SEE II Corinthians 10:3-6.

    c. Four categories of the enemy:

        1.

        2.

        3.

        4. Spiritual Wickedness in high places: Earthly activities

Note # 4: Activities of Spiritual Wickedness

Wicked spirits in the earth's atmosphere work to destroy all that is of Jesus Christ.

1. Hindering

2. Blinding

3. Deceiving

4. Tempting

5. Beating

6. Tempting

6:13 Wherefore take unto you the whole armor of God, that ye may be able to withstand in the evil day, and having done all, to stand.

   a. Paul repeats the command to take/put on the whole armor of God (SEE vs 11)

   b. Only God's armor can defend us in spiritual warfare

   c. If we do not withstand the devil's attack, we are not using all the armor that God has made available to us

   d. "Having done all to stand" means that protection is not automatic. God requires our cooperation in the battle.

6:14 Stand therefore, having your loins girt about with truth, and having on the breastplate of righteousness;

6:15 And your feet shod with the preparation of the gospel of peace.

6:16 Above all, taking the shield of faith, wherewith ye shall be able to search all the fiery darts of the wicked one.

6:17 And take the helmet of salvation, and the sword of the Spirit, which is the word of do.

6:18 <u>Praying always</u> with all prayer and supplication in the Spirit, and watching thereunto with all perseverance and supplication for all saints;

    a. The voice of our victory – Prayer

    b. The power to prevail – Prayer –"always"

Note #5: Seven Pieces of Armor

1.

2.

3.

4.

5.

6.

7.

6:19 And for me, that utterance may be given unto me, that I may open my mouth boldly, to make known the mystery of the gospel.

6:20 For which I am an ambassador in bonds: that therein I My speak boldly, as I ought to speak.

    a. Paul requests prayer

        a. For utterance (words) that he may preach the gospel with power

        b. Arrest, beatings, imprisonment, threat of death – nothing deterred Paul from the call of God

        c. Paul's desire and prayer was that men might be saved (SEE Ro 10:1)

    b. Paul did not see himself as a prisoner, but as an "ambassador in bonds". Our faith must be based on God's kingdom principles, not man's.
SEE Ep 4:1; 2 Timothy 1:8; *Philemon 1:9*

6:21 But that ye also may know my affairs, and how I do, Tychicus, a beloved brother and faithful minister is the Lord, shall make known to you all things

6:22 Whom I have sent unto you for the same purpose that ye might know our affairs, and that he might comfort your hearts.

    a. Tychicus is serving Paul as his messenger, delivering the letter to the Ephesians, inform them about Paul and comfort them.

    b. Tychicus was with Paul in Rome when Paul was imprisoned.

6:23 Peace be to the brethren and love and with faith, from God the Father and the Lord Jesus Christ.

6:24 Grace be with all them that love our Lord Jesus Christ in sincerity. Amen.

    a. Paul's triple blessing reminding us of the abundance of blessings we have from God.
    b. Grace was the main revelation that God gave Paul.

Note #6: The Work of the Holy Spirit: (12 References)

Chapters 1-3: Who the Holy Spirit is and Does for the Believer.

1.

2.

3.

4.

5.

Chapters 4-6: What the Believer should do for the Spirit.

1.

2.

3.

4.

5.

6.

7.

8.

Note #7: Christ's love for the Church in Ephesians 5:25-33:

Past:

Present:

Future:

PART TWO

PAUL'S LETTER TO THE PHILIPPIANS

AUTHOR: Paul

   Paul clearly identifies himself as the writer, 1:1

DATE: Early 60s A.D. during Paul's first Roman imprisonment

   Clearly Paul was in prison (1:7, 13,17), probably Rome, but some think perhaps Caesarea, A.D. 59-61, or Ephesus, A.D. 54.

THEME: Letter of Joy, a Thank you letter

   The Philippian church had sent Paul money and also one of their members, Epaphroditus, to help take care of Paul's needs (2:25; 4:10,14-19)

WRITTEN TO: Philippi to thank, encourage and instruct.

   Epaphroditus had been very ill but was recovered and able to take Paul's letter home.

KEY PEOPLE: Paul, Epaphroditus, Timothy

SECTION 2.1 THE CITY OF PHILIPPI

a. Located nine miles from the Aegean Sea, northwest of the island of Thasos, in a fertile plain, near the seaport of Neapolis.

b. Philip of Macedon, father of Alexander the Great, took Philippi in 358 B.C., from the empire of Thrace to whom it originally belonged. He built the city and named it for himself.

c. Philippi became a prominent city of Rome because it was on the Via Egnatia, the main road from Rome to the province of Asia, regarded as "the chief city of that part of Macedonia, a colony" (Acts 16:12).

d. Roman colonies were distinctively Roman and proud of it, which may explain why the citizens complained against Paul concerning customs contrary to Romans(Acts 16:21-26). The people saw themselves as Romans.

e. There was no synagogue in Philippi, which indicates there was not a significant Jewish population. This was a contrast to large numbers of Jews in other Greek cities such as Corinth, Berea, Athens, and Thessalonica. Many former Roman soldiers lived there.

   f. Philippi was Paul's first European church. He crossed the Aegean Sea and took the Gospel to the people in this Macedonian city, after having a night vision and hearing someone say, "Come over into Macedonia, and help us" (Acts 16:9). Silas and Timothy went with him.

SECTION 2.2 OVERVIEW

   a. Introduction (1:1-11)

   b. News (1:12-26)

   c. Encouragement and Instruction (1:27-2:18)

   d. Plans for Timothy and Epaphroditus (2:19-30)

   e. Warnings against enemies and dangers (3:1-4:9)

   f. Paul's final Thank You (4:10-20)

   g. Conclusion (4:21-23)

SECTION 2.3 HISTORICAL SETTING OF THE PHILIPPIAN LETTER:

During Paul's second missionary journey, The Lord called Paul to preach the gospel in Macedonia. Acts 16:8-10 "And they passing by Mysia came down to Troas. (9) And a vision appeared to Paul in the night; there stood a man of Macedonia, and prayed him, saying, Come over into Macedonia, and help us. (10) And after he had seen the vision, immediately we endeavored to go into Macedonia, assuredly gathering that the Lord had called us for to preach the gospel unto them.)

The city of Philippi evidently had no synagogue, so Paul went outside the city to the river bank to preach. There he found Lydia and a number of other women, who received the word of the Lord and came to faith in Christ. Acts 16:11-14 "Therefore loosing from Troas, we came with a straight course to Samothracia, and the next day to

Neapolis; (12) And from thence to Philippi, which is the chief city of that part of Macedonia, and a colony: and we were in that city abiding certain days. (13) And on the Sabbath we went out of the city by a river side, where prayer was wont to be made; and we sat down, and spake unto the women which resorted thither. (14) And a certain woman named Lydia, a seller of purple, of the city of Thyatira, which worshiped God, heard us: whose heart the Lord opened, that she attended unto the things which were spoken of Paul.

Lydia and her family were baptized, and she invited Paul and his traveling companions to stay at her house. Acts 16:15 "And when she was baptized, and her household, she besought us, saying, If ye have judged me to be faithful to the Lord, come into my house, and abide there. And she constrained us."

Later, Paul and Silas were arrested and put in prison in Philippi, because they cast an unclean spirit out of a girl who had been following them, driven by the devil. Acts 16:16-25 "...as we went to prayer, a certain damsel possessed with a spirit of divination met us...(17) the same followed Paul and us, and cried, saying, These men are the servants of the most high God, which show unto us the way of salvation. (18)...Paul, being grieved, turned and said to the spirit, I command thee in the name of Jesus Christ to come out of her. And he came out the same hour. (19) And when her masters saw that the hope of their gains was gone, they caught Paul and Silas, and drew them into the marketplace unto the rulers...(23) And when they had laid many stripes upon them, they cast them into prison, charging the jailor to keep them safely...(25) And at midnight Paul and Silas prayed, and sang praises unto God: and the prisoners heard them (26) And suddenly there was a great earthquake, so that the foundations of the prison were shaken: and immediately all the doors were opened, and every one's bands were loosed... (27) and the keeper of the prison awaking out of his sleep...(29) sprang in, and came trembling, and fell down before Paul and Silas, (30) And brought them out, and said, Sirs, what must I do to be saved? (31) And they said, Believe on the Lord Jesus Christ, and thou shalt be saved, and thy house... (34) And when he (the jailor) had brought them into his house, he set meat before them, and rejoiced, believing in God with all his house. (35) And when it was day the magistrates sent the sergeants, saying, Let those men go."

Paul may have visited Philippi again when he traveled from Ephesus to Macedonia. He stayed with them in the spring. Acts 20:1,6 "And after the uproar was ceased, Paul called unto him the disciples, and embraced them, and departed for to go into Macedonia. (2) And when he had gone over those parts, and had given them much exhortation, he came into Greece, (3) And there abode three months...(6) And we sailed away from Philippi after the days of unleavened bread, and came unto them to Troas in five days; where we abode seven days. 2 Corinthians 2:12,13 "When I came to Troas to preach Christ's gospel, and a door was opened unto me of the Lord, (13) I had no rest in my spirit, because I found not Titus my brother: but taking my leave of them, I went from thence into Macedonia."

The church in Philippi was probably the first church in all of Europe. Paul usually refused to accept financial assistance from churches. 2 Corinthians 11:7-9 "Have

I committed an offense in abasing myself that ye might be exalted, because I have preached to you the gospel of God freely? (8) I robed other churches, taking wages of them, to do you service. (9) And when I was present with you, and wanted, I was chargeable to no man: for that which was lacking to me the brethren which came from Macedonia supplied [Philippians]: and in all things I have kept myself from being burdensome unto you, and so will I keep myself." Paul did accept gifts from the Philippians when he was in Thessalonica. And Epaphroditus brought another gift to Paul during his imprisonment in Rome. Philippians 4:16-18, "For even in Thessalonica ye sent once and again unto my necessity. (18) But I have all, and abound: I am full, having received of Epaphroditus the things which were sent from you, an odor of a sweet smell, a sacrifice acceptable, well-pleasing to God." While Epaphroditus was in Rome visiting Paul, he became very sick and nearly died. He did recover, however, and carried the Philippian letter back home. Philippians 2:25-30 "I supposed it necessary to send to you Epaphroditus, my brother, and companion in labor, and fellow soldier, but your messenger, and he that ministered to my wants. (26) For he longed after you all, and was full of heaviness, because that ye had heard that he had been sick. (27) For indeed he was sick nigh unto death: but God had mercy on him. (30) for the work of Christ he was nigh unto death, not regarding his life, to supply your lack of service toward me."

SECTION 2.4 KEY VERSE

Philippians 4:4
Rejoice in the Lord always: and again I say, Rejoice.

SECTION 2.5 TEXT: PAUL'S LETTER TO THE PHILIPPIANS

CHAPTER ONE:

Introduction and Greeting (1:1-2)

1:1 Paul and Timothy, the servants of Jesus Christ, to all the saints in Christ Jesus which are at Philippi, with the bishops and deacons:

   a. Timothy is included in the greeting because he ministered with Paul in Philippi and knew these people well
   b. Paul's identity was in who he served
   c. Believers are elevated to "saints" because of what Jesus did for us. There is no basis for limiting sainthood to a few elite believers
   d. "bishops and deacons" were the leaders in Philippian church

1:2 Grace be unto you, and peace, from God our Father, and from the Lord Jesus Christ.

   a. Grace and Peace always go together
   b. SEE Romans 5:1-5

Paul's Prayer for the Philippian Church (1:3-11)

1:3 I thank my God upon every remembrance of you,

1:4 Always in every prayer of mine for you all making request with joy,

1:5 For your fellowship in the gospel from the first day until now;

   a. The Philippians were some of Paul's closets friends
   b. They had supported him more than any other church (Ph 4:15-16)

1:6 Being confident of this very thing, that he which hath begun a good work in you will perform it until the day of Jesus Christ:

   a. Pauls confidence was that God continues to work in the lives of his children
   b. Success is not automatic, it requires our cooperation

1:7 Even as it is meet for me to think this of you all, because I have you in my heart; inasmuch as both in my bonds, and in the defense and confirmation of the gospel, ye all are partakers of my grace.

      a. Paul had confidence in the grace of God because of his own experience
      b. They had partaken of the same grace

1:8 For God is my record, how greatly I long after you all in the bowels of Jesus Christ.

      a. God is the one who really knows and can testify to the truthfulness of what is in Paul's heart
      b. SEE Romans 1:9; 2 Corinthians 1:23; I /Thessalonians 2:5,10
      c. "bowels" = tender mercies (NIV)

1:9 And this I pray, that your love may abound yet more and more in knowledge and in all judgment;

      a. SEE 2 Peter 1:3 all things that pertain unto life and godliness, through the knowledge of him
      b. Even love is based on knowledge, spiritual understanding

1:10 That ye may approve things that are excellent; that ye may be sincere and without offense till the day of Christ;

1:11 Being filled with the fruits of righteousness, which are by Jesus Christ, unto the glory and praise of God.

      a. That "you may be able to discern what is best" (NIV)
      b. Spiritual knowledge gives us better understanding of right and wrong
      c. Fruits of righteousness follow understanding and discerning of spirits

Paul Knows His Life Circumstances Advance the Gospel (1:12-30)

1:12 But I would ye should understand, brethren, that the things which happened unto me have fallen out rather unto the furtherance of the gospel;

1:13 So that my bonds in Christ are manifest in all the palace, and in all other places;

1:14 And many of the brethren in the Lord, waxing confident by my bonds, are much more bold to speak the word without fear.

    a. Paul, as a prisoner himself, is comforting his friends who are free
    b. He helps them look at his bonds as he does, as advancing the kingdom of God
    c. His imprisonment gave opportunity to share the gospel with all the soldiers of the emperor's house in Rome
    d. His imprisonment also encouraged others to be more bold in the gospel

1:15 Some indeed preach Christ even of envy and strife; and some also of good will:

1:16 The one preach Christ of contention, not sincerely, supposing to add affliction to my bonds:

1:17 But the other of love, knowing that I am set for the defense of the gospel.

1:18 What then? Notwithstanding, every way, whether in pretence, or in truth Christ is preached; and I therein do rejoice, yea, and will rejoice.

    a. Different motives for ministry – envy and strife or pure motives
    b. Paul rejoices anyway, for it is the Word that works, not the messenger.

1:19 For I know that this shall turn to my salvation through your prayer, and the supply of the Spirit of Jesus Christ,

1:20 According to my earnest expectation and my hope, that in nothing I shall be ashamed, but that with all boldness, as always, so now also Christ shall be magnified in my body, whether it be by life, or by death.

1:21 For to me to live is Christ, and to die is gain.

    a. "salvation" = Gr. "soteria", which means rescue or safety
    b. Can refer to physical or spiritual salvation
    c. There are rewards for those who endure persecution for the gospel's sake (Mt 10:40-42)

1:22 But if I live in the flesh, this is the fruit of my labor: yet what I shall choose I wot not.

1:23 For I am in a strait between two, having a desire to depart, and to be with Christ; which is far better:

1:24 Nevertheless to abide in the flesh is more needful for you.

1:25 And having this confidence, I know that I shall abide and continue with you all for your furtherance and joy of faith;

    a. Paul's purpose was to be sold out to Jesus Christ, to focus all his attention, to be consumed with the Lord
    b. Paul longed to be with Jesus, but

1:26 That your rejoicing may be more abundant in Jesus Christ for me by my coming to you again.

    a. Paul knew the Philippians would be very happy to see him again in person
    b. Paul did not live in false humility (pride) but simply knew he was somebody in Christ Jesus, somebody the Philippians loved

1:27 Only let your conversation be as it becometh the gospel of Christ: that whether I come and see you, or else be absent, I may hear of your affairs, that ye stand fast in one spirit, with one mind striving together for the faith of the gospel;

    a. Conversation = behavior, manner of life, conduct (habit and lifestyle)
    b. Paul is encouraging his friends to sincerely live for Christ

1:28 And in nothing terrified by your adversaries: which is to them an evident token of perdition, but to you of salvation and that of God.

1:29 For unto you it is given in the behalf of Christ, not only to believe on him, but also to suffer for his sake;

1:30 Having the same conflict which ye saw in me, and now hear to be in me.

CHAPTER TWO

Christlikeness (2:1-4)

2:1 If there be therefore any consolation in Christ, if any comfort of love, if any fellowship of the Spirit, if any bowels and mercies,

2:2 Fulfill ye my joy, that ye be likeminded, having the same love, being of one accord, of one mind.

2:3 Let nothing be done through strife or vainglory; but in lowliness of mind let each esteem other better than themselves.

2:4 Look not every man on his own things, but every man also on the things of others.

    a. "if" is used four times for emphasis, (Greek " since"), not to ask a question
    b. since God has done so much for us, let us be like Him and love one another
    c. The cure for self-centeredness is esteeming others higher than himself.
    d. Look at life from another's point of view.

Christ's Life (2:5-11)

2:5 Let this mind be in you, which was also in Christ Jesus:

    a. understood subject of the sentence is "you"
    b. indicates it is our choice to let his mind (attitude) work in us
    c. indicates an inward state of mind rather than outward thinking

2:6 Who, being in the form of God, thought it not robbery to be equal with God:

2:7 But made himself of no reputation, and took upon him the form of a servant, and was made in the likeness of men:

2:8 And being found in fashion as a man, he humbled himself, and became obedient unto death, even the death of the cross.

2:9 Wherefore God also hath highly exalted him, and given him a name which is above every name:

2:10 That at the name of Jesus every knee should bow, of things in heaven and things in earth, and things under the earth;

2:11 And that every tongue should confess that Jesus Christ is Lord, to the glory of God the Father.

    a. Jesus is God the Son (Jn 1:1)
    b. Humbled himself and laid aside his divinity to identify with mankind forever!
    c. Jesus humbled himself even unto death.

2:12 Wherefore, my beloved, as ye have always obeyed, not as in my presence only, but now much more in my absence, work out your own salvation with fear and trembling.

    a. Paul encourages steadfastness in living for God.
    b. Work "out" your own salvation, the salvation which begins in the spirit, a gift of God, received by faith

2:13 For it is God which worketh in you both to will and to do of his good pleasure.

    a. God leads us and guides us into His will
    b. We must cooperate and choose his way. We must work (walk) it out.

2:14 Do all things without murmurings and disputings:

2:15 That ye may be blameless and harmless, the sons of God, without rebuke, in the midst of a crooked and perverse nation, among whom ye shine as lights in the world;

2:16 Holding forth the word of life; that I may rejoice in the day of Christ, that I have not run in vain neither labored in vain.

    a. without complaining, muttering, or secret displeasure
    b. from the root of doubting

2:17 Yea, and if I be offered upon the sacrifice and service of your faith, I joy and rejoice with you all.

2:18 For the same cause also do ye joy, and rejoice with me.

- a. Paul testified that he would rejoice if martyred for the gospel
- b. Paul further wanted the Philippians to rejoice for him if he was martyred, as one who obtains a better resurrection (He 11:35)

Paul Sends Timothy

2:19 But I trust in the Lord Jesus to send Timothy shortly unto you, that I also may be of good comfort, when I know your state.

2:20 For I have no man likeminded, who will naturally care for your state.

2:21 For all seek their own, not the things which are Jesus Christ's.

2:22 But ye know the proof of him, that, as a son with the father, he hath served with me in the gospel.

2:23 Him therefore I hope to send presently, so soon as I shall see how it will go with me.

2:24 But I trust in the Lord that I also myself shall come shortly.

- a. Paul put the needs of the Philippians above his own, even during his imprisonment when he needed help the most
- b. Paul generously sent them his most trusted companion, Timothy
- c. Paul is waiting to see what sentence Caesar would hand down, so Timothy could inform his friends in Philippi.
- d. There are differences of opinion as to whether Paul got out of this imprisonment (SEE Acts 28:30). *Paul expected to be released.*

Paul sends Epaphroditus back to Philippi

2:25 Yet I supposed it necessary to send to you Epaphroditus, my brother, and companion in labor, and fellow soldier, but your messenger, and he that ministered to my wants.

2:26 For he longed after you all, and was full of heaviness, because that ye had heard that he had been sick.

2:27 For indeed he was sick nigh unto death: but God had mercy on him; and not on him only, but on me also, lest I should have sorrow upon sorrow.

2:28 I sent him therefore the more carefully, that when ye see him again, ye may rejoice, and that I may be the less sorrowful.

2:29 Receive him therefore in the Lord with all gladness; and hold such in reputation:

2:30 Because for the work of Christ he was nigh unto death, not regarding his life, to supply your lack of service toward me.

    a. Epaphroditus means "lovely". It is believed he carried the Philippian letter.
    b. He became sick because of his service to Paul in the ministry.
    c. His name is mentioned twice in the New Testament, 2:25 and 4:18.
    d. Paul sent Epaphroditus back to Philippi to reassure his friends that he had been healed.
    e. He could assure them of his health, and share with them Paul's situation.

CHAPTER THREE

Our Standing Before God

3:1 Finally my brethren, rejoice in the Lord. To write the same things to you, to me indeed is not grievous, but for you it is safe.

   a. "Joy" and "rejoice" are used 17 times in this letter
   b. Paul exhorts to rejoice as a habit and lifestyle, not dependent on circumstances

3:2 Beware of dogs, beware of evil workers, beware of the concision.

3:3 For we are the circumcision, which worship God in the spirit, and rejoice in Christ Jesus, and have no confidence in the flesh.

   a. "concision" (to mutilate) is a play on words to "circumcision"
   b. legalistic circumcision to obtain salvation was nothing more than mutilation, for it had no saving power.

3:4 Though I might also have confidence in the flesh. If any other man thinketh that he hath whereof he might trust in the flesh, I more:

3:5 Circumcised the eighth day, of the stock of Israel, of the tribe of Benjamin, a Hebrew of the Hebrews; as touching the law a Pharisee;

3:6 Concerning zeal, persecuting the church; touching the righteousness which is in the law, blameless.

3:7 But what things were gain to me, those I counted loss for Christ.

3:8 Yea doubtless, and I count all things but loss for the excellency of the knowledge of Christ Jesus my Lord: for whom I have suffered the loss of all things, and do count them but dung, that I may win Christ,

3:9 And be found in him, not having mine own righteousness, which is of the law, but that which is through the faith of Christ, the righteousness which is of God by faith:

   a. Salvation is a condition of the heart and not the flesh
   b. Those who trust the law of circumcision are putting confidence in the flesh to save them, rather than in God.

3:10 That I may know him, and the power of his resurrection, and the fellowship of his sufferings, being made conformable unto his death;

3:11 If by any means I might attain unto the resurrection of the dead.

Pressing Toward the Mark for the Prize of Christ Jesus

3:12 Not as though I had already attained, either were already perfect: but I follow after, if that I may apprehend that for which also I am apprehended of Christ Jesus.

3:13 Brethren, I count not myself to have apprehended: but this one thing I do, forgetting those things which are behind, and reaching forth unto those things which are before,

3:14 I press toward the mark for the prize of the high calling of God in Christ Jesus.

3:15 Let us therefore, as many as be perfect, be thus minded: and if in any thing ye be otherwise minded, God shall reveal even this unto you.

   a. Paul had given up everything, naturally speaking, to know (Gr. Ginosko) Jesus Christ. The Greek word means an intimate knowing like a husband knows his wife.
   b. Paul didn't want to know about Christ, but to know him intimately.
   c. Paul stated that when we serve the Lord in sincerity, God will reveal any areas of shortcomings to us.

3:16 Nevertheless, whereto we have already attained, let us walk by the same rule, let us mind the same things.

3:17 Brethren, be followers together of me, and mark them which walk so as ye have us for an example.

      a. Paul emphasized progress, growth, and winning
      b. He wanted his friends in Philippi to fervently follow the Lord in all things.
      c. Paul was telling them to "mark" or take aim at godly examples of living.

3:18 (For many walk, of whom I have told you often, and now tell you even weeping, that they are the enemies of the cross of Christ:

3:19 Whose end is destruction, whose God is their belly, and whose glory is in their shame, who mind earthly things.)

      a. Those who act as their own Savior are the enemies of God, They ignore the salvation provided by the death, burial and resurrection of Jesus Christ, and live for themselves.
      b. SEE Romans 8:6 "to be carnally minded is death."

3:20 For our conversation is in heaven; from whence also we look for the Savior, the Lord Jesus Christ:

3:21 Who shall change our vile body, that it may be fashioned like unto his glorious body, according to the working whereby he is able even to subdue all things unto himself.

      a. Paul declares that his lifestyle (conversation) is as a citizen of heaven, one who looks for the return of the Lord Jesus Christ.
      b. Paul had his eyes on the big picture, the "end of our faith"

CHAPTER FOUR

Rejoice in the Lord (4:1-9)

4:1 Therefore, my brethren dearly beloved and longed for, my joy and crown, so stand fast I the Lord, my dearly beloved.

- a. "therefore" (in view of) refers to the previous verses, in which Paul speaks of our future glorification, how God will "change our vile body, that it may be fashioned like unto his glorious body"
- b. We should live in light of the glorious reward of the future

4:2 I beseech Euodias, and beseech Syntyche, that they be of the same mind in the Lord.

4:3 And I entreat thee also, true yokefellow, help those women which labored with me in the gospel, with Clement also, and with other my fellow laborers, whose names are in the book of life.

- a. Euodias (fragrant) and Syntyche (with fate) were two women in the Philippian church who had labored with Paul in the gospel (v 3).
- b. Evidently they had had a disagreement, and Paul was encouraging them to be reconciled in the Lord.

4:4 Rejoice in the Lord always: and again I say, Rejoice.

- a. Paul's admonition is to rejoice always, at all times. It is not only possible, but preferable.
- b. Most people do not rejoice because they do not recognize the fruit of the Spirit within them (Galatians 5:22)

4:5 Let your moderation be known unto all men. The Lord is at hand.

    a. "moderation" = Greek, "epieikes", also translated gentlness (NIV), forbearing (NAS), unselfishness, considerateness (AMP) and patient.
    b. Jesus is coming soon. Let us live with that in view.

4:6 Be careful for nothing; but in every thing by prayer and supplication with thanksgiving let your requests be made known unto God.

    a. "Careful" means "full of care and anxiety".
    b. Paul admonishes us to rejoice, which keeps our focus on the Lord and His promises.

4:7 And the peace of God, which passeth all understanding, shall keep your hearts and minds through Christ Jesus.

    a. peace comes as a result of our casting our care upon him (I Pe 5:7)
    b. Those who carry burdens have not totally cast their care (Is 26:3; La 3:51)

4:8 Finally, brethren, whatsoever things are true, whatsoever things are honest, whatsoever things are just, whatsoever things are pure, whatsoever things are lovely, whatsoever things are of good report; if there be any virtue, and if there be any praise, think on these things.

    a. Focus on eight positive areas of thinking
    b. Thinking right leads to living right

Note #8: Eight Positive Areas of Thinking

1.

2.

3.

4.

5.

6.

7.

8.

4:9 Those things, which ye have both learned, and received, and heard, and seen in me, do: and the God of peace shall be with you.

    a. Paul reverses the order of disciples' learning: "learned, received, heard, seen"
    b. He begins from where they are and walks backward through the process of how they grew in faith

Note #9: Progression of a Transformed Life

1.

2.

3.

4.

Paul's Contentment and Thanksgiving (4:10-20)

4:10 But I rejoiced in the Lord greatly, that now at the last your care of me hath flourished again; wherein ye were also careful, but ye lacked opportunity.

4:11 Not that I speak in respect of want: for I have learned, in whatsoever state I am, therewith to be content.

4:12 I know both how to be abased, and I know how to abound: everywhere and in all things I am instructed both to abound and to suffer need.

4:13 I can do all things through Christ which strengtheneth me.

4:14 Notwithstanding ye have well done, that ye did communicate with my affliction.

4:15 Now ye Philippians know also, that in the beginning of the gospel, when I departed from Macedonia, no church communicated with me as concerning giving and receiving, but ye only.

4:16 For even in Thessalonica ye sent once and again unto my necessity.

4:17 Not because I desire a gift: but I desire fruit that may abound to your account.

4:18 But I have all, and abound: I am full, having received of Epaphroditus the things which were sent from you, an odor of a sweet smell, a sacrifice acceptable, well-pleasing to God.

    a. Paul received offerings from the Philippians on more than one occasion (SEE 4:10, 15,16,18)
    b. Paul's intentions with the Corinthian church had been misunderstood (I Co 9:11-13). Some thought he would not receive offerings from anyone he ministered to, but this was not accurate.

4:19 But my God shall supply all your need according to his riches in glory by Christ Jesus.

   a. Paul is encouraging the Philippians who had given to the gospel, and by doing so had made deposits in their heavenly account (you cannot outgive God)
   b. God uses our generosity to multiply our giving back to our own needs. (SEE Mt 7:7-12)

4:20 Now unto God and our Father be glory forever and ever. Amen.

Paul Signs the Letter with Final Greetings (4:21-23)

4:21 Salute every saint in Christ Jesus. The brethren which are with me greet you.

4:22 All the saints salute you, chiefly they that are of Caesar's household.

   a. Paul greets all those who belong to Jesus Christ as "saints".
   b. Those of Caesar's household probably refers to servants Paul reached for the Lord, in the palace of Caesar. (SEE Ph 1:12-13)

4:23 The grace of our Lord Jesus Christ be with you all. Amen.

   a. Grace and peace are gifts from God (Ep 2:8-10; Ro 5:1-5)
   b. Grace and peace can be multiplied through the knowledge of God (2 Pe 1:2)

PART THREE

PAUL'S LETTER TO THE COLOSSIANS

AUTHOR: Paul, included Timothy as a co-laborer

DATE: Early 60s A.D. during Paul's first Roman imprisonment

THEME: Divine supremacy sufficiency of Christ, and warnings against false teaching

The theme and content of the Colossian letter are very similar to the Ephesian letter. Ephesians focuses on the Church (body). Colossians focuses of the Christ (head).

WRITTEN TO: Saints (Christians) and faithful at Colosse

OTHER KEY PEOPLE: Paul, Tychicus, Onesimus

SECTION 3.1 THE CITY OF COLOSSE

a. The city of Colosse was 14 miles from Laodicea (one of the seven churches addressed in Revelation 1:4; 3:14-22). Colosse was 100 miles southeast of Ephesus, and close to Hirapolis (Co 4:13).
b. Colosse was relatively insignificant. In the valley of the Lycos river, it was on the main trade route from Ephesus to the east.
c. In A.D. 61, there was an earthquake in the Lycus Valley. Laodicea suffered the greatest damage. It is mentioned four times in the Colossian letter, as well as in Revelation (Co 2:1; 4:13,15,16; Re 1:11; 3:14). Colosse had been a prominent city, but was in decline in the time of Paul, overshadowed by the rebuilding of Laodicea and Hierapolis.
d. Colosse thrived into the second and third centuries A.D. before it was devastated by an earthuake, and most of its population moved several miles south to Chonai (modern Honaz).

SECTION 3.2 THE HISTORICAL SETTING OF THE LETTER

a. Paul never visited the city of Colosse (Col 2:1). The church there was probably founded by Epaphras, a convert of Paul's (1:7-8; 4:12), during the three years Paul was in Ephesus (SEE Acts 19:10)

b. Epaphras had reported to Paul that the church at Colosse was infiltrated by false teachers, declaring a dangerous doctrine that Jesus was neither central to salvation, nor supreme.

c. These false teachers were adding to the gospel the traditions and commandments of men (Mk 7:7). They declared it was necessary to observe certain Jewish rules and regulations (Col 2:16), and to worship angels in a prominent way (Col 2:18).

d. Paul wrote to correct the errors in teaching, and declare that Christ is all sufficient and all –supreme, the only way, the only hope, of salvation and eternal life.

Note#10:Three Marks of a Cult as described in Colossians
(Col 2:6-23)

1. False – must worship certain spiritual powers (More interest in angels or spirit beings than in Jesus Christ)

2. False – must submit to circumcision (Superiority; ordinary believers scorned)

3. False – must observe set festival days (Great importance of festivals and disciplines rather than relationship with God)

e. The faith of young Christians was threatened, and so Paul wrote to bring correction and encouragement to faithfulness to Jesus Christ.
f. Paul's Response: Christ is All-Sufficient!
g. Paul was in prison when he wrote this letter (4:18).

SECTION 3.3 COMPARISON OF COLOSSIAN AND EPHESIAN LETTERS

a. Scholars have noted that 78 out of the 95 verses in Colossians are similar to Ephesians.
b. Tychicus (with Onesimus accompanying him) delivered both letters.
c. Both letters were written A.D. 61-64 from Paul while in a Roman prison.
d. The greetings in each are similar.
e. The structure of the letters is similar.

Note #11: Corresponding Verses in Ephesians and Colossians

a. Ephesians   Colossians

1.7   1.14

1:10   1:20

1:22   1:18

1:23   2:9

6:21   4:7

SECTION 3.3 TEXT: PAUL'S LETTER TO THE COLOSSIANS

CHAPTER ONE

Greetings to the Saints at Colosse

1:1 Paul, an apostle of Jesus Christ by the will of God, and Timothy our brother,

1:2 To the saints and faithful brethren in Christ which are at Colosse: Grace be unto you, and peace, from Go our Father and the Lord Jesus Christ.

Thanksgiving Prayer: The Progress of the Gospel

1:3 We give thanks to God and the Father of our Lord Jesus Christ, praying always for you,

1:4 Since we heard of your faith in Christ Jesus, and of the love which ye have to all the saints.

    a. Every prayer should begin and end with Thanksgiving (SEE Mt 6:9-13)
    b. The love of Christ saves us, and causes us to reach out to others (SEE Ro 2:4; I Jn 4:20).

1:5 For the hope which is laid up for you in heaven whereof ye heard before in the word of the truth of the gospel;

1:6 Which is come unto you, as it is in all the world; and bringeth forth fruit, as it doth also in you, since the day ye heard of it, and knew the grace of God in truth:

1:7 As ye also learned of Epaphras our dear fellow servant, who is for you a faithful minister of Christ;

    a. The Colossians had heard and received the gospel, which gives such wonderful hope for the future that it affects the way we live our present lives.
    b. The gospel is the message for all mankind, the Good News from God to every people, tribe, tongue and nation in the world. (SEE Jn 3:16)
    c. Epaphras is mentioned three times in the New Testament:

        1. Col 1:7 "our dear fellow servant, who is for you a faithful minister of Christ"

        2. Col 4:12 "one of you, a servant of Christ"

        3. Phile 1:23 "my fellow prisoner in Christ Jesus" [It is not known if Epaphras was actually in prison with Paul, or if this is a reference to him as a fellow believer.

    d. These references imply that Epaphras was the one who brought the gospel to Colosse.

1:8 Who also declared unto us your love in the Spirit.

1:9 For this cause we also, since the day we heard it, do to cease to pray for you, and to desire that ye might be filled with the knowledge of his will in all wisdom and spiritual understanding;

1:10 That ye might walk worthy of the Lord unto all pleasing, being fruitful in every good work and increasing in the knowledge of God;

1:11 Strengthened with all might, according to his glorious power, unto all patience and longsuffering with joyfulness;

    a. The apostles were given to prayer, and to the teaching and preaching of God's Word (Acts 6:4)
    b. Paul desires is that the Colossians be filled with the knowledge of God's will
    c. Being filled results in the blessings of vs 10-11

1:12 Giving thanks unto the Father, which hath made us meet to be partakers of the inheritance of the saints in light:

1:13 Who hath delivered us from the power of darkness and hath translated us into the kingdom of his dear Son:

1:14 In whom we have redemption through his blood, even the forgiveness of sins:

   a. God "hath" made us meet to be partakers. He has already done it.
   b. "meet" = Greek, Hikanoo, which means "to make sufficient or render fit"
   c. NIV says "has qualified you", SEE John 1:12
   d. "redemption" = Greek, Apolytrosis, which means "a buying back, a setting free by paying a ransom price" (Ro 3:24; 8:23; I Co 1:30)
   e. "through his blood" – His blood sacrifice was so great that it outweighed all our sins, the sins of the whole world (Jn 3;16; Ro 4:8)

The Preeminence of Christ (1:15-23)

1:15 Who is the image of the invisible God, and firstborn of every creature:

   a. Jesus is the express, perfect image of the Father (He 1:3)
   b. Jesus is the "image" =He fully represents the Father in actions, nature, and character (Jn 14:9)

1:16 For by him were all things created, that are in heaven, and that are in earth, visible and invisible, whether they be thrones, or dominions, or principalities, or powers: all things were created by him, and for him:

   a. Four levels of authority include physical and spiritual kingdoms
   b. All was created by him, and for him (Re 4:11)

1:17 And he is before all things, and by him all things consist.

1:18 And he is the head of the body, the church: who is the beginning, the firstborn from the dead; that in all things he might have the preeminence.

      a. Jesus Christ is head of the Church, his body (Ep 1:22-23)
      b. "the beginning" does not refer to Christ having a beginning, but refers to his resurrection. He was the beginning of a new people who did not exist before, the new creations (2 Co 5:17)

1:19 For it pleased the Father that in him should all fullness dwell;

      a. Jesus is preeminent because He is the Creator (v 17)
      b. Jesus is the creator of things in heaven and earth (v 16), whether visible or invisible, the material universe, and all thrones, principalities, dominions, and powers, including angels.
      c. Jesus is not an angel, but creator of angels, who must worship him (He 1:6)

1:20 And, having made peace through the blood of his cross, by him to reconcile all things unto himself; by him, I say, whether they be things in earth, or things in heaven.

      a. SEE Romans 5:1-5; 2 Co 5:17
      b. The ministry of reconciliation to those who will receive it, excluding unrepentant men and fallen angels. Satan's kingdom is under the earth (Ph 2:10)

1:21 And you, that were sometime alienated and enemies in your mind by wicked works, yet now hath he reconciled

1:22 In the body of his flesh through death, to present you holy and unblameable and unreprovable in his sight:

1:23 If ye continue in the faith grounded and settled, and be not moved away from the hope of the gospel, which ye have heard, and which was preached to every creature which is under heaven; whereof I Paul am made a minister;

      a. Separation from God is in our minds first (Ja 1:14)
      b. The renewing of our minds is part of our restoration to all that God purchased for us (Ro 12:1-3)

Exhortation to Steadfastness

1:24 who now rejoice in my sufferings for you, and fill up that which is behind of the afflictions of Christ I my flesh for his body's sake, which is the church:

   a. "afflictions" means "pressure" (Greek, Thlipsis)
   b. Afflictions can be any pressures which come against us because of our decisions to live for Jesus Christ

1:25 Whereof I am made a minister, according to the dispensation of God which is given to me for you, to fulfill the word of God;

1:26 Even the mystery which hath been hid from ages and from generations, but now is made manifest to his saints:

   a. The mystery was hidden from Old Covenant generations
   b. The mystery is revealed by divine revelation (I Co 2:9-10)
   c. "manifest" means "to render apparent" (Greek, Phaneroo)

1:27 To whom God would make known what is the riches of the glory of this mystery among the Gentiles; which is Christ in you, the hope of glory:

   a. God wants us to have full knowledge, not merely surface knowledge, the "riches of the glory of this mystery"
   b. The mystery that Christ is not only with us, but IN us (2 Co 5:17; Ro 8:9; I Co 6:19, Ep 2:22)

1:28 Whom we preach warning every man, and teaching every man in all wisdom; that we may present every man perfect in Christ Jesus:

1:29 Whereunto I also labor, striving according to his working, which worketh in me mightily.

CHAPTER TWO

Warnings Against Errors

2:1 For I would that ye knew what great conflict I have for you, and for them at Laodicea, and for as many as have not seen my face in the flesh;

   a. Paul's conflict came from his love for them, and desire for their maturity
   b. Paul's conflict was in prayer (SEE Galatians 4:19)

2:2 That their hearts might be comforted, being knit together in love and unto all riches of the full assurance of understanding, to the acknowledgement of the mystery of God, and of the Father, and of Christ;

   a. Paul was writing to clarify and ground the Colossians in the fundamentals of faith.
   b. They had not heard from him directly, nor seen his face "in the flesh" (2:1)

2:3 In whom are hid all the treasures of wisdom and knowledge.

   a. "In whom" refers to Christ himself (Ep 1:18-20)
   b. He is in us (Ro 8:9; I Jn 4:15) and we are in him (2 Co 5:17), so then, all the "treasures of wisdom and knowledge" (Ph 4:19) of God is in us through Him, and can be drawn out by understanding.

2:4 And this I say, lest any man should beguile you with enticing words.

2:5 For though I be absent in the flesh, yet am I with you in the spirit, joying and beholding your order, and the steadfastness of your faith in Christ.

2:6 As ye have therefore received Christ Jesus the Lord, so walk ye in him:

2:7 Rooted and built up in him, and established in the faith, as ye have been taught, abounding therein with thanksgiving.

2:8 Beware lest any man spoil you through philosophy and vain deceit, after the tradition of men, after the rudiments of the world, and not after Christ.

   a. "Beware" – be on guard. Be grounded in the faith so no man can move you away.
   b. "spoil" (Greek, Sulagogeo, "to carry off booty…as captive; lead away from the truth)
   c. Satan's only weapon is deception… "beguile you" (I Pe 5:8)

2:9 For in him dwelleth all the fullness of the Godhead bodily.

   a. Another reference to the deity of Jesus Christ.
   b. See I Timothy 3:16
   c. "Godhead" is found 3 times in New Testament (Acts 17;29; Ro 1:20; Co 2:9)
   d. Pantheistic view of Paul's day was that God is in everything, nature as well as man, but Paul uses the word "theotes, which literally means "Deity, the state of being God" (Thayer).
   e. Plural name for God, Elohim, is used over 2700 times in the Old Testament.

2:10 And ye are complete in him, which is the head of all principality and power:

   a. Knowledge of completeness in Christ is our safeguard against deception.
   b. Revelation of what we have in Christ should be our driving hunger. Satisfaction in our life in Christ disarms Satan's lies.

2:11 In whom also ye are circumcised with the circumcision made without hands, in putting off the body of the sins of the flesh by the circumcision of Christ:

2:12 Buried with him in baptism, wherein also ye are risen with him through the faith of the operation of God, who hath raised him from the dead.

2:13 And you, being dead in your sins and the uncircumcision of your flesh, hath he quickened together with him, having forgiven you all trespasses;

    a. Old Testament circumcision was a private act between man and God, and so pictures spiritual circumcision (2:11)
    b. Uncircumcised were identified as unholy and unclean (Is 52:1; Ez 44:7-9)
    c. "dead in your sins" = spiritual death
    d. "forgiven you all trespasses" = our wonderful benefits of salvation!

2:14 Blotting out the handwriting of ordinances that was against us, which was contrary to us, and took it out of the way, nailing it to his cross;

    a. Paul's reference is to the ink and paper used in his day as an example of the forgiveness of sin
    b. Ink could be totally blotted away from the paper, it did not soal in permanently.

2:15 And having spoiled principalities and powers, he made a show of them openly, triumphing over them in it.

    a. "spoiled" = Greek, Apekduomai, which meanss "to divest wholly, despoil, to strip. Jesus totally stripped Satan of his powers.
    b. The picture is of a conquered foe, paraded in defeat and shame, naked and powerless.
    c. Satan has no real power, only the power we give him through his deception.
    d. SEE Ep 6:11; 2 Co 11:14; Col 1:13; Mt 24:4

2:16 Let no man therefore judge you in meat, or in drink, or in respect of al holy day, or of the new moon, or of the Sabbath days:

2:17 Which are a shadow of things to come; but the body is of Christ.

    a. The New Covenant brings all men together in Christ, irregardless of religious tradition or ordinances.
    b. All have equal access to God (Ep 2:14-15, 18)

2:18 Let no man beguile you of your reward in a voluntary humility and worshiping of angels, intruding into those things which he hath not seen, vainly puffed up by his fleshly mind.

    a. Paul is saying "Do not be deceived. There is no reward in mere self denial or in worshipping angels."

2:19 And not holding the Head, from which all the body by joints and hands having nourishment ministered, and knit together, increaseth with the increase of God.

    a. Jesus is preeminent in all things.
    b. Jesus is above all ritual or tradition of men (Mk 7:7)
    c. Jesus is the Head of the body of Christ (I Co 12:14, 27) The church is his body, and functions under his direction.

Legalism

2:20 Wherefore if ye be dead with Christ from the rudiments of the world, why, as though living in the world, are ye subject to ordinances,

2:21 (Touch not; taste not; handle not;)

2:22 Which all are to perish with the using; after the commandments and doctrines of men?

2:23 Which things have indeed a show of wisdom in will-worship, and humility, and neglecting of the body; not in any honor to the satisfying of the flesh.

    a. All our rules and regulations about religion are the commandments of men.
    b. Jesus summed it all up in commands to love God and to love men (SEE Mt 22:36-39; I Jn 3:23)

CHAPTER THREE

Renewed in Knowledge

3:1 If ye then be risen with Christ, seek those things which are above, where Christ sitteth on the right hand of God.

3:2 Set your affection on things above, not on things on the earth.

3:3 For ye are dead, and your life is hid with Christ in God.

3:4 When Christ who is our life, shall appear, then shall ye also appear with him in glory.

   a. "Since" you are born again, a child of God, focus on heavenly realities
   b. "Since" you are dead to the world and risen with Christ (Ro 6:5), focus on heavenly things, not earthly things
   c. Think, seek, meditate, read – focus your affections in His kingdom
   d. Knowledge is power – the resurrection power of Jesus Christ released into our lives

3:5 Mortify therefore your members which are upon the earth; fornication, uncleanness, inordinate affection, evil concupiscence, and covetousness, which is idolatry:

   a. Paul gives practical expression to his instructions (SEE Ga 5:19)
   b. Sin attacks our humanity, we must trust God and yield ourselves to him.

3:6 For which things' sake the wrath of God cometh on the children of disobedience:

3:7 In the which ye also walked some time, when ye lived in them.

   a. The children of disobedience are unbelievers
   b. Paul speaks to believers as being separate from children of disobedience

3:8 But now ye also put off all these; anger, wrath, malice, blasphemy, filthy communication out of your mouth.

3:9 Lie not one to another, seeing that ye have put off the old man with his deeds;

3:10 And have put on the new man, which is renewed in knowledge after the image of him that created him:

    a. Every Christian has a spiritual mind (1 Co 2:16 "the mind of Christ")
    b. Every Christian has a physical mind (1 Co 2:14)

3:11 Where there is neither Greek nor Jew, circumcision nor uncircumcision, Barbarian, Scythian, bond nor free: but Christ is all, and in all.

    a. Paul says to "put off" sins of the flesh (Greek, Apotithemi, same as putting off clothes)
    b. Putting off of the "old man" or old way of life (3:9)
    c. Putting on of the "new man" (3:10)

3:12 Put on therefore, as the elect of God, holy and beloved, bowels of mercies, kindness, humbleness of mind, meekness, longsuffering;

    a. We are born again while dead in trespasses and sins, by repenting, or turning away from sin, and receiving the gift of salvation through Jesus Christ. (Ep 2:1)
    b. As the new man begins to flex his muscles, the effects of the old man are diminished (Ro 6:6)

3:13 Forbearing one another, and forgiving one another, if any man have a quarrel against any: even as Christ forgave you, so also do ye.

    a. Colossians 3:8-13 is very much like Ephesians 4:22-32

3:14 And above all these things put on charity, which is the bond of perfectness.

    a. "above" = upon, on or over, the idea of putting on something, like clothes
    b. Love covers everything (1 Co 13; 1 Pe 4:8)
    c. "love" = Greek, Agape, the God-kind of love.

3:15 And let the peace of God rule in your heats, to the which also ye are called in one body; and be ye thankful.

    a. let = to grant permission, allow
    b. rule = umpire, Greek, Brabeuo, to arbitrate, to govern
    c. thankful (1 Thessalonians 5:18)

3:16 Let the word of Christ dwell in you richly in all wisdom; teaching and admonishing one another in psalms and hymns and spiritual songs, singing with grace in your hearts to the Lord.

3:17 And whatsoever ye do in word or deed, do all in the name of the Lord Jesus, giving thanks to God and the Father by him.

    a. not merely memorizing scripture, but allowing the Holy Spirit to inspire our understanding "richly"
    b. we are priests, ministers, unto the Lord (1 Pe 1:9; Mt 1; Ex 19)
    c. psalms hymns, and spiritual songs (Ps 100; 22; 40; 148)
    d. We stand before God for man
    e. We stand before man for God

Domestic Duties in Home Life

3:18 Wives, submit yourselves unto your own husbands, as it is fit in the Lord.

3:19 Husbands, love your wives, and be not bitter against them.

3:20 Children, obey your parents in all things: for this is well pleasing unto the Lord.

3:21 Fathers, provoke not your children to anger, lest they be discouranged.

3:22 Servants, obey in all things your masters according to the flesh; not with eyeservice, as menpleasers; but in singleness of heart, fearing God:

3:23 And whatsoever ye do, do it heartily, as to the Lord, and not unto men;

3:24 Knowing that of the Lord ye shall receive the reward of the inheritance; for ye serve the Lord Christ.

3:25 But he that doeth wrong shall receive for the wrong which he hath done; and there is no respect of persons.

CHAPTER FOUR

Various Admonitions

4:1 masters, give unto your servants that which is just and equal; knowing that ye also have a Master I heaven.

    a. Col 3:18-4:1 is similar to Ephesians 5:22-33 and 6:1-9
    b. Paul talks about mutual submission in marriage; Wives submit to husbands (1 Co 11:3) "as is fit in the Lord" (3:18-19; Ep 5:25)
    c. Children to parents (4:20; Ep 6:1)
    d. Parents to children (4:21; Ep 6:4)
    e. Servants to Masters (Employees to Employers) (4:22; Ep 6:5)

4:2 Continue in prayer and watch in the same with thanksgiving;

4:3 Withal praying also for us, that God would open unto us a door of utterance, to speak the mystery of Christ, for which I am also I bonds:

4:4 That I may make it manifest, as I ought to speak.

4:5 Walk in wisdom toward them that are without, redeeming the time.

4:6 Let your speech be always with grace, seasoned with salt, that ye may know how ye ought to answer every man.

    a. Paul exhorts the Colossians to watch and pray with thanksgiving, the foundations of communication with God. (4:2)
    b. Paul requests prayer for his ministry team (4:3)
    c. Paul encourages his friends to walk in wisdom toward unbelievers (4:5) NIV says "Be wise in the way you acts toward outsiders; make the most of every opportunity."
    d. Speak in a godly way, always pointing others toward Christ (4:6)

4:7 All my state shall Tychicus declare unto you, who is a beloved brother, and a faithful minister and fellow servant in the Lord:

4:8 Whom I have sent unto you for the same purpose, that he might know your estate, and comfort your hearts;

4:9 With Onesimus, a faithful and beloved brother, who is one of you. They shall make known unto you all things which are done here.

   a. Tychicus brought the letter to the Colossians, and would deliver Paul's heart of love and concern, along with news of Paul's situation
   b. Tychicus would get an update on the church and return the report to Paul
   c. Onesimus, (means profitable, useful). He was the runaway slave of Philemon, and was a Colossian. He was converted by Paul to the gospel, and traveled with Tychicus.

4:10 Aristarchus my fellow prisoner saluteth you, and Marcus, sister's son to Barnabas, (touching whom ye received commandments: if he come unto you, receive him;)

4:11 And Jesus, which is called Justus, who are of the circumcision. These only are my fellow workers unto the kingdom of God, which have been a comfort unto me.

4:12 Epaphras, who is one of you, a servant of Christ, saluteth you, always laboring fervently for you in prayers, that ye may stand perfect and complete in all the will of God.

4:13 For I bear him record, that he hath a great zeal for you, and them that are in Laodicea, and them in Hierapolis.

4:14 Luke, the beloved physician and Demas, greet you.

- a. (4:10) Aristarchus was from Thessalonica (Acts 27:2); accompanied Paul on his third missionary journey (Acts 19:29; 20:4)
- b. Marcus is John Mark, a cousin to Barnabas; accompanied Paul on first missionary journey (Acts 12:25)
- c. Justus, comforted Paul during his imprisonment in Rome
- d. Epaphras, a Colossian, perhaps founder of the church there
- e. Luke, one of the original twelve disciples of the Lord; traveled everywhere with Paul
- f. Demas, traveled with Paul but later left him.
- g. Nymphas, only mention in scripture, means "given, or born."

4:15 Salute the brethren which are in Laodicea, and Nymphas, and the church which is in his house.

4:16 And when this epistle is read among you, cause that it be read also in the church of the Laodiceans; and that ye likewise read the epistle from Laodicea.

- a. That Paul wanted them to share the letter shows that anyone may benefit from Paul's instructions concerning the truth of the gospel
- b. Paul's letter was full of truth for all men at all times

4:17 And say to Archippus, Take heed to the ministry which thou hast received in the Lord that thou fulfill it.

- a. Thought by some to be the son of Philemon (Phile 1:2).
- b. Archippus means "horse-ruler"
- c. Paul may have been giving a warning, or simply exhorting Archippus to continue in the ministry given him by God.

4:18 The salutation by the hand of me Paul. Remember my bonds. Grace be with you. Amen.

- a. Paul usually wrote by secretarial help.
- b. Tertius was his secretary in Rome (Romans 16:22).
- c. At the end of the letter Paul signed his signature, which helped prevent forgeries to be passed around as if from Paul.
- **d.** "Remember my bonds." This brief statement is full of information as well as a request for prayer. Paul was not complaining, but realistically asking for prayer concerning his imprisonment, and its impact on his work.

PART FOUR

PAUL'S LETTER TO PHILEMON

AUTHOR: Paul

DATE: Early 60s A.D. during Paul's first Roman imprisonment, at about the same time as Ephesians, Colossians, and Philippians were written

THEME: A plea for mercy and forgiveness for Onesimus, a runaway slave
This is the most personal of all Paul's letters, but was written as an apostolic letter about a personal matter. It was intended for others to read.

WRITTEN TO: Philemon, a wealthy member of the Colossian church

KEY PEOPLE: Paul, Philemon, Onesimus

SECTION 4.1 HISTORICAL SETTING OF PHILEMON

Paul, a prisoner of Rome under house arrest, met Onesimus, a runaway slave. According to the Law of Moses, Paul did not betray him as a fugitive, nor did he write to Philemon to come and take Onesimus back. Rather, Paul gave the slave shelter in his own house. Also, Paul shared the gospel with Onesimus, who received the word of God and prayed the saving prayer of repentance (Philemon 1:10).

Paul then sent Onesimus back to Philemon, carrying the letter from Paul with a request for the slave's freedom (Phile1:12 "receive him, that is, mine own bowels"). Paul declared that the slave's escape had occurred by the merciful providence of God, and that Onesimus should receive him not as a servant, but as a brother in Christ (Phile1:15-17).

Some scholars suggest that Onesimus had stolen something from his master and had run away to avoid being punished. This could be so, because Paul offered to repay any debt that Onesimus owed Philemon (Phile 1:18 "If he hath wronged thee, or oweth thee aught, put that on mine account"). Traditionally it is believed that Philemon did as Paul requested, received Onesimus as a brother in the faith, and forgave his debt (Phile 1:21).

SECTION 4.2 OVERVIEW OF THE LETTER

a. Ancient cultures, Roman, Greek, and Jewish, existed within many class barriers, as society told people to stay in their place – men and women, slave and free, rich and poor, Jew and Gentile, Greeks and barbarians, religious and heathen.

b. The message of Jesus Christ brings the walls down, and Paul declared, *"Where there is neither Greek nor Jew, circumcision nor uncircumcision, Barbarian, Scythian, bond nor fee: but Christ is all, and in all" (Col 3:11).*

c. Onesimus "belonged" to Philemon, a wealthy member of the church at Colosse, and a close friend of Paul.

d. Onesimus probably had stolen from Philemon, and had run away, ending up in Rome by the providence of God. There he met Paul, who welcomed him and preached the gospel to him (Phili 1:10). Onesimus received the word and was born again through Paul's ministry.

e. Paul wrote to Philemon to explain what had happened, and to ask Philemon to receive Onesimus back, not as a slave, but as a brother in the Lord (Phile 1:11,12,16).

f. Paul asked Philemon to forgive Onesimus (Phile 1:10, 14, 15,20, 21)

g. Messenger: Sent by the hand of Onesimus to his master

h. Paul's letter to Philemon is a wonderful example of Christian friendship in action. It stands as an example to the modern church to "strive for the unity of the spirit and the bond of peace" (Ephesians 4:3).

SECTION 4.3 ANALYSIS OF THE BOOK

a. <u>FORGIVENESS</u>: Paul's intercessory letter to Philemon on behalf of Onesimus, a slave, is a picture of Jesus Christ's intercession for us who were slaves to sin.

b. <u>RECONCILIATION</u>: As Paul worked to reconcile Onesimus to his master, Philemon, so Jesus Christ worked to reconcile us to God through himself.

c. <u>RESTITUTION</u>: As Paul offered to pay the debts of Onesimus the slave, so Jesus Christ paid our debt of sin.

d. <u>RESTORATION</u>: As Onesimus returned to his master, so we must return to our Master to serve him, and be received in love by our heavenly father.

SECTION 4.4 TEXT: PAUL'S LETTER TO PHILEMON

CHAPTER ONE:

1:1 Paul, a prisoner of Jesus Christ, and Timothy our brother, unto Philemon our dearly beloved, and fellow laborer,

1:2 And to our beloved Apphia and Archippus our fellow soldier, and to the church in thy house:

1:3 Grace to you and peace, from God our Father and the Lord Jesus Christ.

a. Paul did not see himself as a prisoner of Rome, but a prisoner for Christ.
b. Timothy was one of Paul's most trusted companions. Timothy's name is included with Paul's in 2 Corinthians, I Thessalonians, 2 Thessalonians, Philippians, Colossians, and Philemon.
c. Philemon was a Greek land owner living in Colosse. He had been converted under the preaching of Paul (possibly in Ephesus).
d. The church at Colosse met in Philemon's home. Church buildings were not common at this time, because of persecutions and expense.
e. Onesimus was one of Philemon's domestic servants.
f. Apphia may have been Philemon's wife.

g. Archippus may have been Philemon's son, or perhaps an elder in the Colossian church. Paul may have included Archippus in the greeting so he would influence Philemon to take Paul's advice.

Paul's Expression of Thanksgiving

1:4 I thank my God, making mention of thee always in my prayers,

1:5 Hearing of thy love and faith, which thou hast toward the Lord Jesus, and toward all saints;

1:6 That the communication of thy faith may become effectual by the acknowledging of every good thing which is in you in Christ Jesus.

1:7 For we have great joy and consolation in thy love, because the bowels of the saints are refreshed by thee, brother.

    a. Philemon had shown love and generosity toward his brothers and sisters in the faith (1:4,5). (SEE He 6:10)
    b. Philemon had also refreshed and ministered to Paul
    c. Paul set the stage for his request for Onesimus by encouraging Philemon to take account of his ministry and remember what Jesus had provided through the Cross.

Onesimus

1:8 Wherefore, though I might be much bold in Christ to enjoin thee that which is convenient,

1:9 Yet for love's sake I rather beseech thee, being such a one as Paul the aged, and now also a prisoner of Jesus Christ.

    a. Paul based his request not on his apostolic authority, but on Philemon's Christian commitment. Paul wanted to encourage true, heartfelt obedience.
    b. Paul built reconciliation by rebuilding trust:

        1. Paul identified with both Philemon "my brother" (1:7) and Onesimus "my son" (1:10)
        2. Paul appealed to Philemon without making demands.
        3. Paul encouraged Philemon to voluntarily forgive and receive Onesimus.
        4. Paul appealed through love, not authority.
        5. Paul offered to make personal restitution of Onesimus' debts to Philemon.

1:10 I beseech thee for my son Onesimus, whom I have begotten in my bonds:

    a. Philemon had the right to kill Onesimus as punishment.
    b. Paul helped Philemon see the slave as a brother in the Lord, going even beyond forgiveness, to acceptance. (Mt 6:12; Ep 4:31,32)

1:11 Which in time past was to thee unprofitable, but now profitable to thee and to me:

    a. Onesimus' name means "useful"
    b. Paul used a play on words, "unprofitable" to "profitable"

1:12 Whom I have sent again: thou therefore receive him, that is, mine own bowels:

1:13 Whom I would have retained with me, that in thy stead he might have ministered unto me in the bonds of the gospel:

1:14 But without thy mind would I do nothing; that thy benefit should not be as it were of necessity, but willingly.

1:15 For perhaps he therefore departed for a season that thou shouldest receive him forever;

1:16 Not now as a servant, but above a servant, a brother beloved, especially to me, but how much more unto thee, both in the flesh and in the Lord?

- a. Paul wanted to keep Onesimus with him, but sent him back to Philemon for his benefit
- b. Christian status as a member of God's family makes us all equals in Christ.
- c. Galatians 3:28 "There is neither Jew nor Greek, there is neither bond nor free, there is neither male nor female: for ye are all one in Christ Jesus."
- d. Verses 15,16 KEY VERSES of the book

1:17 If thou count me therefore a partner, receive him as myself.

- a. "partner" means a partner in the grace of God; co-laborers
- b. Paul did not merely tolerate Onesimus, but worked alongside him

1:18 If he hath wronged thee, or oweth thee aught, put that on mine account;

- a. Paul showed love for Onesimus by offering to pay his debts
- b. Paul's heart was to encourage both Onesimus and Philemon, and he stood between them as a minister of reconciliation and restoration

1:19 I Paul have written it with mine own hand, I will repay it: albeit I do not say to thee how thou owest unto me even thine own self besides.

1:20 Yea, brother, let me have joy of thee in the Lord: refresh my bowels in the Lord.

1:21 Having confidence in thy obedience I wrote unto thee, knowing that thou wilt also do more than I say.

   a. Paul had led Philemon to Christ, so Philemon was also Paul's begotten in the Lord
   b. Paul appealed to Philemon's acknowledgement of the debt of gratitude he owed Paul

1:22 But withal prepare me also a lodging: for I trust that through your prayers I shall be given unto you.

   a. Paul was released from prison soon after writing this letter
   b. It is not known if Paul returned to Colosse to visit the saints

1:23 There salute thee Epaphras, my fellow prisoner in Christ Jesus;

   a. Epaphras was well known to the Colossians. It is believed he founded the church there (Colossians 1:7)
   b. He worked to encourage the Christians there during times of persecution and struggles with teachers of false doctrine.
   c. Epaphras had reported to Paul, which resulted in the letter from Paul to the Colossians.
   d. Epaphras may have been in prison with Paul. (Colossians 4:12,13)

1:24 Marcus, Aristarchus, Demas, Lucas, my fellow laborers.

1:25 The grace of our Lord Jesus Christ be with your spirit. Amen.

   a. These Christians are also mentioned in Colossians 4:10,14
   b. Mark is "John Mark" who accompanied Paul on his first missionary journey, and also wrote the Gospel of Mark.
   c. Aristarchus traveled with Paul and is called his "fellow-prisoner" implying he may have been imprisoned for the gospel too. (Acts 19:29; 20:4; 27:2; Col 4:10)
   d. Demas had been faithful to Paul but later deserted him (2 Timothy 4:10)
   e. Lucas (Luke) had accompanied Paul on his third missionary journey. Luke was a physician, and wrote the Gospel of Luke and the book of Acts.

BIBLIOGRAPHY

Baxter, J. Sidlow. Explore the Book. Zondervan Publishing House, Grand Rapids, Michigan. 1960, 1966 in one volume.

Briscoe, Stuart. Bible Study Tool Kit. InterVarsity Press, 1991.

Hendriksen, William. New Testament Commentary. Galatians and Ephesians. Baker Book House, Grand Rapids, Michigan. 1968, ninth printing, July 1994.

Key Word Study Bible. KJV. Spiros Zodhiates, Th.D., Exe. Editor. AMG Publishers, Chattanooga, TN 1984, 1991.

Knight, George W. and Rayburn W. Ray. The Illustrated Everyday Bible Companion. Barbour Publishing, Inc. Uhrichsville, Ohio, 2005.

Life Application Bible. NIV. Tyndale House Publishers, Wheaton, Illinois and Zondervan Publishing, Grand Rapids, Michigan. 1997, revised and updated through 2005.

Lockyer, Herbert. All the Men of the Bible. Zondervan Publishing House, 1958.

Thayer, Joseph H. D.D. Thayer's Greek-English Lexicon of the New Testament. Baker Book House. Grand Rapids, Michigan, 1977.

Thompson Chain-Reference Bible. Frank Charles Thompson, D.D., Ph.D., Editor. B.B. Kirkbride Bible Company, Inc. Indianapolis, Indiana, 1988. 10th printing, May 2003.

Wommack, Andrew. Life for Today Study Bible and Commentary. The Galatians, Ephesians, Philippians, and Colossians Edition. Andrew Wommack Ministries, 1998.

ADDENDUM

REVIEW QUESTIONS

REVIEW QUESTIONS ASSIGNMENT #1
Part One – Ephesians Chapters 1-3

1. The church at Ephesus was founded by _____ on his _____ missionary journey.

2. Under Paul's ministry, _____ became the pastor at Ephesus.

3. Paul addressed his letter to Ephesus, rather than to personal friends, because the letter was intended to be _____ throughout the area.

4. Summarize the KEY VERSE of Ephesians: _____
   _____

5. Name 5 words or phrases that emphasize the theme of unity in Ephesians:
   1. _____
   2. _____
   3. _____
   4. _____
   5. _____

6. Paul's letter that is most similar to Ephesians in theme and emphasis is _____.

7. Although UNITY is the overall theme of Ephesians, the book breaks easily into two areas of emphasis, _____ and _____.

8. The first three chapters of Ephesians emphasize the _____ of the believer, which is _____.

9. The last three chapters of Ephesians emphasize the _____ of the believer, which is not doctrinal so much as _____.

10. Ephesians 1:3 illustrates the doctrinal truth of the _____ of the believer.

11. Ephesians 4:1 illustrates the practical truth of the believer's _____.

12. What is the two-part message of Ephesians Chapter One?
    (1) _____
    (2) _____

13. What is the two-part message of Ephesians Chapter Two?
    _____
    _____

14. What is the two-part message of Ephesians Chapter Three?
    _____
    _____

15. Another way to view and study the book of Ephesians, according to Dr. Riley, Is to see the book in _____.

16. Summarize the 3-fold "source of our salvation" in Ephesians 1:1-18
    1. 1:4-6 _____
    2. 1:7-12 _____
    3. 1:13-14 _____

17. Paul prayed for Man's spiritual knowledge in Ephesians 1:15-18, to understand the
    1. _____ of Prayer
    2. _____ of Prayer

18. Discuss the 3-fold "manifestation of God's power" in Ephesians 1:19-2:22
    1. in relation to _____
    2. in relation to _____
    3. in relation to _____

19. What is the 3-fold understanding of God's power in relation to Christ according to Ephesians 1:19-23?
    1. concerning His _____
    2. concerning His _____
    3. concerning His _____

20. What is the 3-fold understanding of God's power in relation to the individual according to Ephesians 2:1-10?
    1. 2:1-5 concerning spiritual _____
    2. 2:6 concerning spiritual _____
    3. 2:7-10 concerning spiritual _____

21. What is the 3-fold understanding of God's power in relation to humanity?
    1. 2:11-13 concerning the _____
    2. 2:14-17 concerning the _____
    3. 2:19-22 concerning the _____

22. Discuss Paul's 3-fold "statement about himself" in Ephesians 3:1-21
    1. 3:1-12 _____
    2. 3:13-19 _____
    3. 3:20-21 _____

REVIEW QUESTIONS ASSIGNMENT #2
Part One – Ephesians Chapters 4-6

1. What is the overall theme of discipleship in Ephesians chapters 4,5, and 6?
   _____

2. In Ephesians 4:1-16, Paul begins to discuss three aspects of _____.

3. Describe the three areas of unity mentioned by Paul in Ephesians 4:1-16
   1. 4:1-3 _____
   2. 4:4-6 _____
   3. 4:7-16 _____

4. This 3-fold approach to unity described in 4:1-16 concerns the_____.

5. Spiritual fruit such as Paul described in his letter to the Galatians, 5:22, describe qualities essential to unity, including

   a. Lowliness, which is
   _____

   b. Meekness, which is
   _____

   c. Long-suffering, which is
   _____

   d. Forbearance, which is _____ and _____

6. Paul describes unity as ONE (1)_____, (2) _____
   (3)_____(4) _____
   (5) _____(6)_____(7)_____.

7. What are two ways we can work to produce unity?
   1. _____
   2. _____

8. What is the purpose of ministry gifts within the Church? _____
   _____
   _____

9. What is exhortation? (1)_____(2)_____

10. Ephesians 4:17-32 gives instruction concerning _____.

11. The walk of the individual Paul teaches is in regards to _____.

12. What is the "old man" of sin we choose to put off? _____

13. What is the "new man" of the spirit? _____

14. What scriptures describe the old man of sin? _____.

15. What scriptures describe the new man of spirit? _____.

16. Ephesians 5:1-20 concerns our New Walk toward _____.

17. Our New Walk toward outsiders (unbelievers) includes
    (1) 5:1-7 _____
    (2) 5:8-14 _____
    (3) 5:15-20 _____

18. Ephesians 5:21-6:9 concerns our New Walk toward _____.

19. Our New Walk toward insiders includes
    (1) 5:21-33 _____
    (2) 6:1-4 _____
    (3) 6:5-9 _____

20. Ephesians 6:10-20 is Paul's instruction concerning walking _____.

21. Three areas of walking in spiritual warfare include
    (1) _____
    (2) _____
    (3) _____

22. Describe POWER in spiritual warfare
    (1) _____
    (2) _____
    (3) _____

23. Describe PRAYER in spiritual warfare
    (1) _____
    (2) _____
    (3) _____

24. Describe PEACE in spiritual warfare
    (1) _____

25. Ephesians chapter four could be summarized as instructions for believers
    (1) 4:1-16 _____
    (2) 4:17-32 _____

26. Ephesians chapter five could be summarized as instructions for believers
    (1) 5:1-20 _____
    (2) 5:21-6:9 _____

27. Ephesians chapter six could be summarized as instructions for believers
    (1) 6:10-24 _____

REVIEW QUESTIONS ASSIGNMENT #3
Part Two – Philippians Chapters 1-4

1. Why are believers elevated to be called "saints"? _____
_____

2. How do we know the Philippian believers were some of Paul's closest friends?
_____

3. God continues to work in us as we _____.

4. Paul's experience and confidence in the grace of God are evident in his
    (1) _____
    (2) _____
    (3) _____

5. In Paul's prayer in chapter 1:3-11, Paul gave thanks for
    (1) _____
    (2) _____
    (3) _____

6. In Philippians 1:9-11, Paul's prayer includes his desire
    (1) _____
    (2) _____
    (3) _____

7. Paul rejoiced in his circumstances mainly because _____
_____.

8. Why did Paul say "...to die is gain"? _____
_____
_____

9. What was the decision Paul faced in Phil 1:22? _____
_____

10. What is our "conversation" in Christ?
    (1) _____
    (2) _____
    _____

11. What does "evident token of perdition" mean in Phil 1:28? _____
_____
_____

12. Give three reasons from Phil 1:1-4 that explain why we should love others
    (1) _____
    (2) _____
    (3) _____

13. What did Paul mean by saying "work out your own salvation" (2:12) and "it is God which worketh in you both to will and to do" (2:13)?
    (1) _____
    (2) _____

14. What did Paul say about complaining and murmuring in Phil 2:14? _____
_____

15. What was Paul's attitude about becoming a martyr for Christ? (2:17-18)
    (1) _____
    (2) _____

16. How did Paul show great leadership under stress while in prison? (2:19)
    (1) _____
    (2) _____

17. Why did Paul send Epaphroditus to Philippi? (2:27)
    (1) _____
_____
    (2) _____

18. What is Paul's emphasis on rejoicing and joy? (3:1) _____
_____

19. Who qualifies as "the circumcision"? 3:3
    (1) _____
    (2) _____
    (3) _____

20. What does Paul mean by saying "that I may win Christ"? 3:8-11
    (1) _____
_____
    (2) _____
    (3) _____

21. When will believers be wholly "perfect"? 3:12 _____
_____

22. What is the "prize of the high calling of God in Christ Jesus"? 3:14 _____
_____
(Hebrews 11:35)

23. What does "perfect" and "thus minded" mean in Phil 3:15?
    (1) _____
    (2) _____

24. What does Paul emphasize for Christians? 3:15
    (1) _____
    (2) _____

25. What did Paul mean by saying "mark them which walk so as ye have us for an example"? 3:17 _____
_____
_____

26. Describe "enemies of the Cross" in 3:18-19 _____
_____
_____
_____

27. What is the NIV definition for "our conversation in Heaven" in Phil 3:20?
_____

28. How is it possible to "rejoice in the Lord always?
    (1) _____
    (2) _____
    (3) _____
    (4) _____

29. How can we "be careful (anxious) for nothing"? 4:6
    (1) _____
    (2) _____

30. Why does Paul emphasize "whatsoever" things? 4:8
_____

31. What is the progression of a transformed life? 4:9
    (1) _____
    (2) _____
    (3) _____
    (4) _____
    (5) _____

32. How do Christians become content in life? 4:11 _____

33. How do Christians do "all things"? 4:13 _____
_____

34. How should we understand Phil 4:19? _____
_____
_____

35. How does God supply our need? 4:19 _____
_____

36. What are the attributes of grace and peace? 4:23
    (1) _____
    (2) _____

REVIEW QUESTIONS ASSIGNMENT #4
Part Three – Colossians Chapters 1-4

1. Why did Paul write the letter to the Colossians? _____

_____

2. The errors Paul was addressing involved a mixture of _____

_____.

3. The pagan philosophy Paul addressed came to be known as _____.

4. Gnostic comes from the Greek word meaning _____.

5. What was the Gnostic view of God's creation? _____

_____

6. Gnosticism is heresy that teaches
    (1) _____
    (2) _____

7. Gnosticism attacked Jesus in His
    (1) _____
    (2) _____
    (3) _____

8. Paul corrected Gnostic error by
    (1) _____
    (2) _____

9. The theme of Colossians can be summed up as _____

_____

10. The pre-eminence of Christ means He is first in
    (1) _____ 1:15-17
    (2) _____ 1:13,14
    (3) _____ 1:19
    (4) _____ 1:20-2:3
    (5) _____
    (6) _____

11. The pastor at Colossae was _____. Col 1:7,8

12. Tychicus, a friend of Paul, delivered letters from Paul in prison to saints at
    (1) _____
    (2) _____
    (3) _____

13. How often did Paul visit Colossae? _____.

14. How may Christians walk worthy of the Lord? Col 1:9 _____

15. What four levels of authority did Paul preach?
    (1) _____
    (2) _____
    (3) _____
    (4) _____

16. How is Jesus Christ pre-eminent in His
    (1) _____
    (2) _____

17. The purpose of our reconciliation from God through Jesus Christ_____.

18. Paul warned believers not to be led astray _____
which is _____ 2:4-7.

19. Paul pointed believers away from Gnosticism to _____.

20. Paul pointed believers away from Legalism and Mysticism to spiritual
    (1) _____ 2:11-12
    (2) _____ 2:13-15
    (3) _____ 2:15-16
    (4) _____ 2:18-19

21. Describe "the old man" 3:5-9 _____

22. Describe "the new man" 3:10-17 _____

23. The messengers who delivered Paul's letter and personal update to the believers at Colossae were
    (1) _____
    (2) _____

24. Who was Onesimus? 4:9 _____

12

REVIEW QUESTIONS ASSIGNMENT #5
Part Four – Philemon Chapter 1

1. When was the letter to Philemon written? _____
_____

2. How does Paul refer to himself in Philemon 1:1? _____
_____

3. Where did Philemon live? How did He know Paul? _____
_____

4. Why did Paul write to Philemon? _____
_____

5. Why is this personal letter included in New Testament scripture? _____
_____

6. Who, besides Philemon, is included in the greeting? _____
_____

7. Where did Paul meet Onesimus? _____

8. Where did the church, of which Philemon was a member, meet? _____
_____

9. What conclusions can be drawn by the fact that the church met in Philemon's house?
    (1)_____
    (2)_____
_____

10. What had Paul heard concerning Philemon? What was Paul's reaction?
    (1)_____
    (2)_____
Paul's reaction: _____
_____

11. What authority did Paul have to command Philemon? (although he didn't use it). Why not? What did Paul do?
    (1)_____
    (2)_____
_____

12. Who was Onesimus? What was his relationship to Philemon? to Paul?
    (1)_____
    (2)_____
    _____

13. Why did Paul say in 1:13? _____
    _____

14. Why did Paul send Onesimus back to Philemon?
    (1)_____
    (2)_____

15. Why did Paul offer to pay any debt that Onesimus may have owed Philemon?
    (1)_____
    _____
    (2)_____
    _____

16. How did Paul encourage Philemon to prayer and looking on the needs of others?
    (1)_____
    (2)_____
    _____

17. What 5 co-laborers joined Paul in saluting Philemon?
    (1) _____
    (2) _____
    (3) _____
    (4) _____
    (5) _____

www.ingramcontent.com/pod-product-compliance
Lightning Source LLC
Chambersburg PA
CBHW080636130526
44591CB00047B/2714